LEARNING WORKS ENRICHMENT SERIES

CASTLES · CODES
CALLIGRAPHY

WRITTEN BY LINDA SPELLMAN
ILLUSTRATED BY BEVERLY ARMSTRONG
CALLIGRAPHY BY RICA COULTER

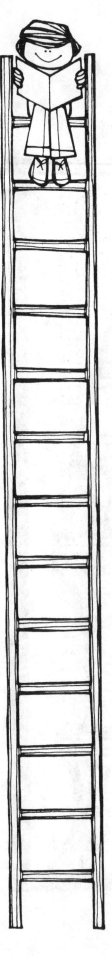

The Learning Works

Edited by Sherri M. Butterfield

Contents

Contents
(continued)

To the Teacher

The activities in this book have been selected especially for gifted students in grades 4 through 6 and are designed to help them develop and apply higher-level thinking skills. These activities have been grouped by subject matter into the following sections: Castles, Codes, and Calligraphy.

Castles

Medieval life with its feudal system, lords, knights, and castles always fascinates the youthful readers of today. On the surface, they view the Middle Ages as a romantic, magical time in history. The activities in this section introduce students to the interesting and often harsh realities of that period. They help students discover how and why castles were built, understand how they were attacked and defended, and learn what life within their walls was like.

Codes

Codes and ciphers have existed for centuries, testing the logic and perseverance of those who have sought to decipher them. They have been simple and complex, written for use by children as well as by adults, and employed in lighthearted games as well as in deadly serious activities. This section includes many coding activities and offers opportunities for divergent as well as convergent thinking.

Calligraphy

In recent years, there has been a resurgence of interest in the art of beautiful handwriting. Calligraphy is now widely used for awards, certificates, and limited-edition books, as well as for personal correspondence. This section gives readers an overview of the tools and materials needed and the correct posture and pen positions for several popular calligraphic styles. It also provides historical background for some of the most well-known alphabets.

JAHO ACKS NOME GHEZ
44.

To the Teacher
(continued)

Within each of these three sections are bulletin board and learning center ideas, a pretest and a posttest, as many as fifteen activity pages, an answer key, and an award to be given to students who satisfactorily complete the unit of study. These materials may be used with your entire class, for small-group instruction, or by individuals working independently at their desks or at learning centers. Although you may want to elaborate on the information presented, each activity has been described so that students can do it without additional instruction.

All of the activities in this book are designed to provide experiences and instruction that are qualitatively different and to promote development and use of higher-level thinking skills. For your convenience, these activities have been coded according to Bloom's taxonomy. The symbols used in this coding process are as follows:

●	**knowledge**	recall of specific bits of information; the student absorbs, remembers, recognizes, and responds.
■	**comprehension**	understanding of communicated material without relating it to other material; the student explains, translates, demonstrates, and interprets.
▲	**application**	using methods, concepts, principles, and theories in new situations; the student solves novel problems, demonstrates use of knowledge, and constructs.
★	**analysis**	breaking down a communication into its constituent elements; the student discusses, uncovers, lists, and dissects.
▬	**synthesis**	putting together constituent elements or parts to form a whole; the student discusses, generalizes, relates, compares, contrasts, and abstracts.
◉	**evaluation**	judging the value of materials and methods given purposes; applying standards and criteria, the student judges and disputes.

These symbols have been placed in the left-hand margin beside the corresponding activity description. Usually, you will find only one symbol; however, some activities involve more than one level of thinking or consist of several parts, each involving a different level. In these instances, several symbols have been used.

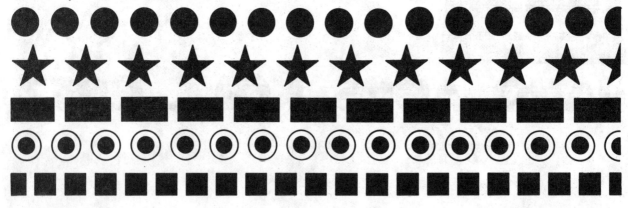

Bulletin Board Ideas

Feudal Pyramid

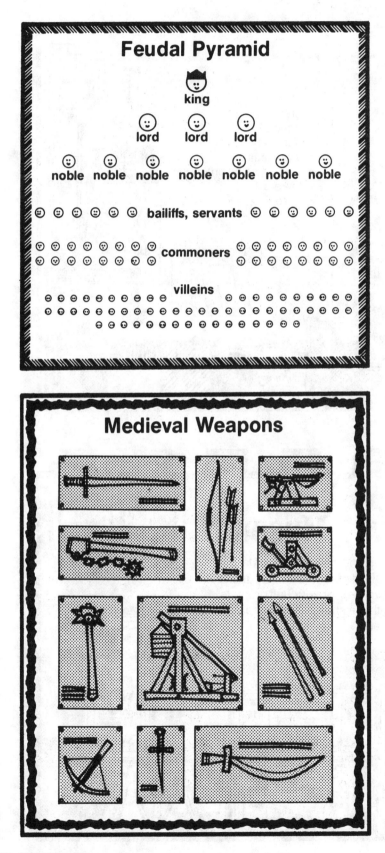

Medieval Weapons

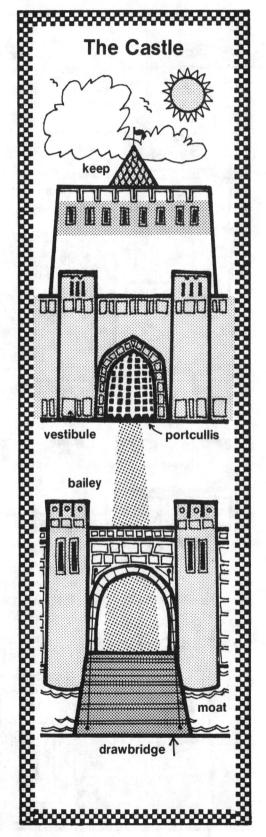

The Castle

Learning Center Ideas

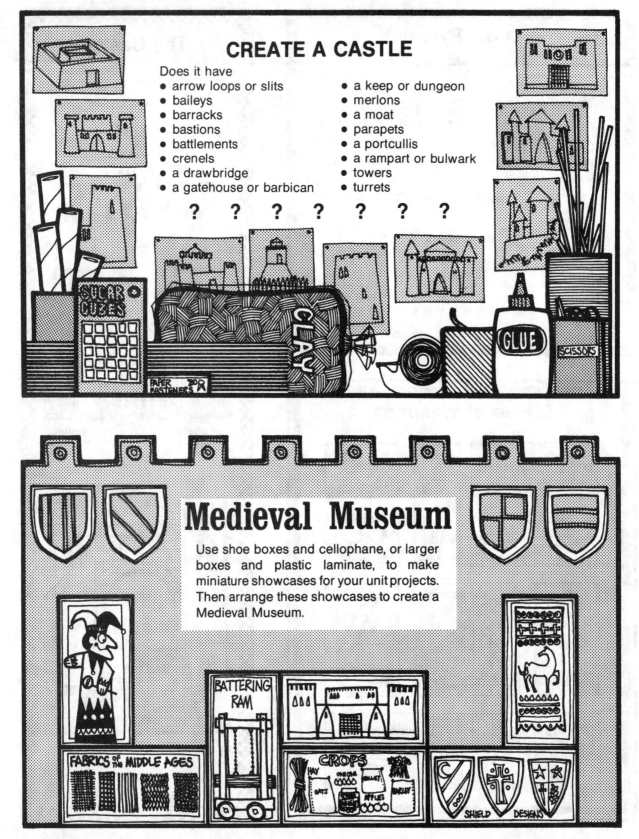

CREATE A CASTLE

Does it have
- arrow loops or slits
- baileys
- barracks
- bastions
- battlements
- crenels
- a drawbridge
- a gatehouse or barbican
- a keep or dungeon
- merlons
- a moat
- parapets
- a portcullis
- a rampart or bulwark
- towers
- turrets

? ? ? ? ? ? ?

SUGAR CUBES

CLAY

PAPER FASTENERS

GLUE

SCISSORS

Medieval Museum

Use shoe boxes and cellophane, or larger boxes and plastic laminate, to make miniature showcases for your unit projects. Then arrange these showcases to create a Medieval Museum.

BATTERING RAM

FABRICS OF THE MIDDLE AGES

CROPS

HAY OATS ONIONS MILLET APPLES BARLEY

SHIELD DESIGNS

Name _____

Pretest

Match the following words with their definitions by writing the correct letter on each line.

_____ 1. bailiff

_____ 2. battlement

_____ 3. catapult

_____ 4. chivalry

_____ 5. crenels

_____ 6. dais

_____ 7. great hall

_____ 8. jester

_____ 9. joust

_____ 10. keep

_____ 11. mail

_____ 12. manor

_____ 13. moat

_____ 14. page

_____ 15. palisade

_____ 16. portcullis

_____ 17. tournament

_____ 18. vassal

_____ 19. villein

_____ 20. wimple

A. the business agent of a feudal lord

B. the main room of a castle keep

C. a large grate made of heavy timbers or iron bars hung by chains over the gateway of a castle and lowered between grooves to prevent unwelcome guests from entering

D. a woman's draped headdress

E. a combat on horseback between two knights with lances

F. a raised platform in a large room or hall

G. armor made of metal chains, links, rings, or plates

H. an estate owned by a feudal lord and consisting of a castle and the land around it

I. a giant slingshot used for throwing large stones, boulders, arrows, spears, and lances

J. a fence of wooden stakes built especially for protection and defense

K. a deep, wide ditch dug around the rampart of a castle and often filled with water

L. one who entertains a king and his court by telling jokes

M. the customs and behavior code of knighthood

N. a loyal servant to a feudal lord

O. a peasant who is a slave to a feudal lord but is free in his legal relations to all others

P. the strongest and most secure part of a castle

Q. a youth who is in personal service to a knight and is being trained for knighthood

R. a festival of contests, games, and jousts

S. a wall with high places to hide behind when you are attacked and low places to look and shoot through when you fight

T. low places in battlements through which you can look and shoot when you fight

Name _____

The Middle Ages

During the third and second centuries B.C., the city of Rome grew strong and extended its control over surrounding areas. In 58 B.C., the Roman general and statesman Julius Caesar conquered the part of Europe that was then known as Gaul. This region included all of what is now France, as well as the northern part of Italy. Three years later, Caesar led his invading armies into Britain. As a result of Caesar's military successes and those of other Roman generals, Rome came to control all of the countries around the Mediterranean Sea and extended its influence as far west as Britain. The city of Rome became an empire.

From 31 B.C. until A.D. 407, the Roman Empire was the most powerful force in all Europe. At the height of its power, Rome exerted great influence on the cultural development of its neighbors. From Rome they took their alphabet, their architecture, their language, and their systems of government and law.

As time went on, Rome grew weak and less able to defend itself against attack. Meanwhile, the Vandals, a savage Germanic tribe from northern Europe, grew strong. During the fourth and fifth centuries A.D., they overran Gaul, Spain, and northern Africa. One by one, they captured Roman cities. City by city, they moved closer to Rome itself. Then, in A.D. 455, as many as eighty thousand Vandals sacked Rome and left the city in ruins. Under the pressure of repeated attacks by barbarians, the Roman Empire collapsed.

For four to six centuries, people had no art, no music, and no education. They lived in fear that they would be attacked by roaming bands of barbarians or would die of the plague or some other dread disease. This sad period is known as the Dark Ages.

About A.D. 800, people began to join together for protection. The strongest warriors among them became kings. Each king took the land he had conquered and divided it among his loyal followers on the condition that they would fight in his army and pay taxes to him. These followers helped the king build a castle in which he and his family could live safely. In case of enemy attack, the king's followers also sought safety within the castle walls. From these sad and savage beginnings came the feudal system and the period known as the Middle Ages.

Activities

1. Make a time line on which you show important dates and events in the rise and fall of the Roman Empire and trace the periods known as the Dark Ages and the Middle Ages.

2. The Vandals were a fierce and savage tribe who plundered and destroyed the cities they invaded. The thoroughness of the destruction that they left in their wake has earned for them a lasting reputation and left its mark on our language. The English words **vandal, vandalism,** and **vandalize** all come from the name of this barbaric tribe. Look up these words. Find out what they mean. Then, relying on what you know about the Vandals, explain why the use of their name in this way is appropriate.

3. Pretend that you are a reporter for the *Rome Register.* Write an account of the invasion of Rome by the Vandals for publication in this newspaper.

Name _____

The Feudal System

The feudal system was much like a pyramid. At the top was a king or a very powerful lord. Under him were a number of **vassals**, lower lords who owed loyalty and service to him. Each of the king's vassals was also a lord with vassals of his own. Sometimes, there were many levels of **liege lords**—lords who had the right to feudal allegiance—and vassals.

Each lord was in charge of a **fiefdom**, which belonged to a more powerful lord or to a king and usually consisted of a castle or fortress and enough surrounding land and forest to supply the needs of the castle. The lord was given the right to collect tolls and taxes from those living on or crossing over his land.

Vassals were required to pay for several items: the cost of any war waged by the lord; the ransom if the liege lord or any members of his family were captured; the cost of knighting the lord's first son; and the expenses associated with the marriage of his eldest daughter. When the lord died, his eldest son inherited his title and control over the fiefdom, but he did have to pay a huge death tax, or **relief**, to his father's liege lord. There were also great payments to be made to the church.

Activities

1. Look up the words **fiefdom**, **liege**, **relief**, and **vassal** in the dictionary. Write down and learn their definitions.
2. Make a chart showing a feudal pyramid.
3. Compare a feudal **relief** with the present-day inheritance tax. In what ways are they alike? In what ways are they different?

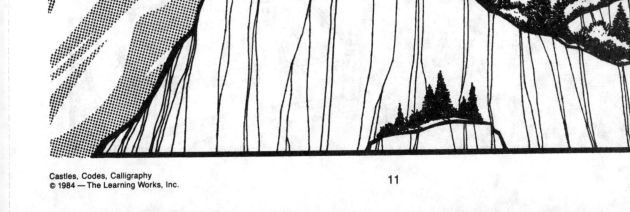

Name _____

The Manor

The fiefdom, or **manor**, was like a small, self-sufficient country. It included the castle; the meadows, fields, and pastures; the mill, stables, and livery; the ovens and kitchens; the rivers and woods; and the church and village. It was peopled by those who carried on the crafts that made it self-sufficient—the butcher, the baker, the candlestick maker, the tinker, the tailor, the cobbler, the blacksmith, and the wine maker.

Other people also lived in the village. They were poor, unpaid peasants who were given strips of land to farm for themselves while working on the lord's fields. These villagers, or **villeins**, lived in mud-and-wood huts with dirt floors, thatched roofs, and one small window. They did all the hard work of the manor—the farming, the constructing, and the repairing. When the manor came under attack, they went to the castle to get protection and to help with the fighting.

A villein belonged to the manor like a slave and was not permitted to leave under normal circumstances. There were, however, several ways for a villein to become free. First, he could claim freedom if he were to escape and avoid capture for one year and one day. Second, if he prospered well, he might possibly be able to buy his freedom. Third, the lord could free him in return for some brave deed he had performed or grant him permission to study religion and enter the service of the church.

The land surrounding the manor was divided into three main sections. One section was for wheat or barley, one for oats, and one lay fallow, or at rest. Each year the crops were rotated so that a different section would lie fallow. Fruits and vegetables were grown on the smaller strips of land. In addition, there was a common pasture for cows and sheep, and pigs were allowed to forage in the woodlands. Of course, if villeins had animals of their own that needed to graze, they had to pay for this privilege.

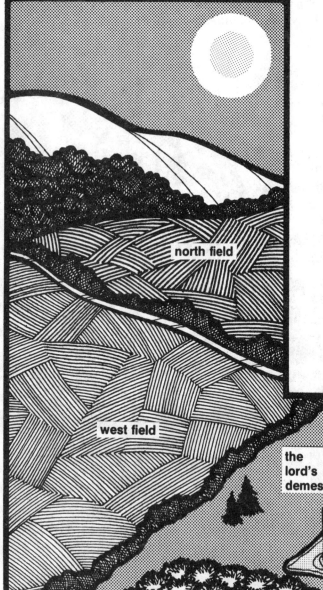

north field

west field

the lord's demesne

Name _____

The Manor
(continued)

The villeins were allowed to grow fruits and vegetables on some of the common land, to bake bread in the lord's oven, to make wine in his wine press, and to grind grain in his mill, but, again, only for a fee.

When there were disagreements on the manor, the lord acted as judge. All fines collected went into his pocket, so often they were higher than was truly fair. In one way or another, the lord managed to keep his pockets full!

Each person's land, whether the lord's or a villein's, was called his **demesne**, and the amount of work he was required to do was his **extent**.

Besides the lord, the manor had three chief officers. The **reeve** was in charge of cultivation of the land, the **bailiff** made sure the work was done and the produce was sold, and the **steward** kept track of the financial accounts.

Activities

▲ 1. Construct a model of a manor or make a map of one.

■ 2. Feudal manors were self-sufficient because each person had a job to do, and each person did his or her job. What might have happened if everyone on the manor had decided to go on strike?

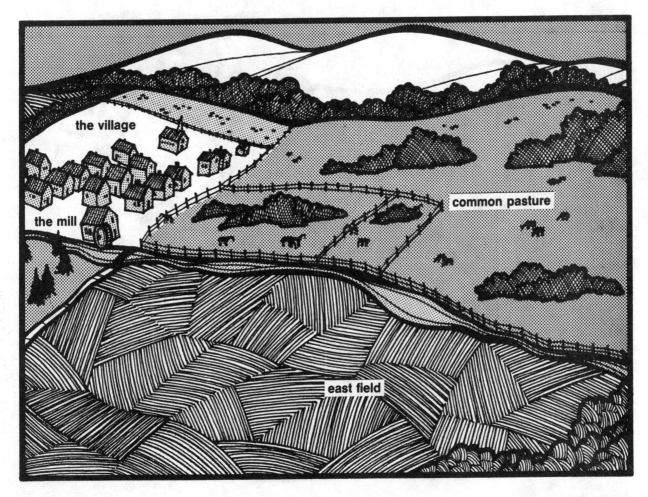

Name _____

Commoners

Commoners were those people who were not part of the nobility or of the church. They were divided into several classes. The **bailiff** was the agent of the lord. His duties included collecting the taxes and managing the fiefdom. The skilled **craftsmen** did all of the production work of the fief and included armorers, bakers, blacksmiths, carpenters, gardeners, horse trainers, leatherworkers, tailors, and weavers. The castle **servants**, including butlers, cooks, maids, pages, and valets, kept the castle running smoothly. The lowest of all commoners were the **peasants**, who were also called **villeins** or **serfs**. Similar to slaves, they were bound to the fief.

Activities

1. Compare the life of a medieval villein, or serf, with the life of an American slave before the Civil War.
2. There are many similarities between the life and social structure of a southern plantation and the life and social structure of a feudal manor. Do some research to learn more about both. Then write a paper in which you compare them. In what ways were they alike? In what ways were they different?
3. Write an editorial either for or against the feudal system. Justify your position.

Early Castles

Originally, a **castle** was any ancient fortress or house with **battlements**. In Roman times, castles were built of dirt. Later, in the Saxon years, they were made of wood. While the purpose of these early structures was to provide protection from invaders, they were not true castles.

The real castle was the private fortress of a lord, king, or noble. It protected the king and his family and followers from invaders and served as a home base for the neighborhood.

The first real castle was a moat-palisade-and-bailey castle. First a large ditch, the **moat**, was dug, and the dirt from it was piled up to make a mound in the middle. At the top of this mound, a strong fence of wooden stakes, called a **palisade,** was built. Within the palisade was a tower, inside of which the lord lived and fought, if the enemy got that close. Early castle towers were not built of stone because the dirt mound could not support the weight. They had no ground floor. Instead, one entered the tower by climbing a ladder, which could be pulled up in times of peril. On the flat ground surrounding the mound was a fenced yard, called a **bailey**, which held other castle buildings.

Activities

▲ 1. Construct a model of an early castle.
■ 2. There are many similarities between the castle palisade and the western fort. Do some research to learn more about both. Then draw and label a picture of each. Be prepared to use these pictures as part of an oral report in which you explain the ways in which these two structures were alike and the ways in which they were different.

Name _____

The Moat-and-Bailey Castle

Kings often had many castles. A castle was the gift of a king to one of his lords and could be kept only so long as the lord paid his taxes, performed his duties, and remained in favor with the king. Some lords had several castles. They lived in one and placed **constables** in charge of the others.

Because of the danger of fire, lords began to do away with palisades. Gradually, these wooden fences were replaced with sturdier stone walls, called **curtains**; and gatehouses, called **barbicans**, were erected at the corners of the curtains. The lords also built stone towers, called **keeps**, or **donjons**, from which we get our word **dungeon**. **Battlements** were added atop the keeps. These structures were walls with high places to hide behind in the event of attack and low places to look and shoot through during battle. The high places were called **merlons**, and the low places were called **crenels**. Slanted foundations, called **plinths**, were added at the bases of the keeps to strengthen them.

The Moat-and-Bailey Castle
(continued)

A forebuilding was often attached to the keep. This structure served as the entry hall, or **vestibule**. It was protected by the **portcullis**. The word portcullis comes from the Middle English words **port** and **colice** and means "sliding door." In a castle, the portcullis was a large grate made of heavy timbers or iron bars. It was set in grooves and hung from chains over the entryway, where it could be lowered to keep unwelcome guests from entering.

portcullis

Activities

▲ 1. Draw and label a detailed floor plan for a moat-and-bailey castle.

▲ 2. Make a working model of a portcullis.

■ 3. Write a real estate ad for a castle being offered for sale. Remember that words cost money. Keep your description brief, but mention the special features of the castle that might appeal to a potential buyer.

Legend

A keep
B portcullis
C drawbridge
D curtain
E inner moat
F inner bailey
G outer bailey
H gatehouse or barbican
I outer moat

double-moated castle

Name _____

Round Keeps

As time went on, keeps were made larger and more complex. The earliest keeps had been square or rectangular, but some later ones were round, or cylindrical. This shape was harder to construct but made the keep easier to defend because there were no corners behind which enemy soldiers could hide and no edges in which they could gain a hand or foot hold. Although few round keeps were built, this shape proved so advantageous that it was adapted for use in castle towers. Massive drumlike towers were placed at either end of the front castle wall. Between them were the portcullis and drawbridge.

Builders not only varied the outer shape of castle structures but also changed the interior arrangement as well. Fancier forebuildings with stairs inside were added to keeps so that visitors to some castles had to climb to a second floor before they could enter the keep. They then had to make yet another climb to reach the great hall.

One castle, the Oxford Castle in England, had three floors—a basement, a lower level, and an upper level. It also had a round main building that was protected by three square towers. One of these towers contained a spiral staircase. Each of the other two towers contained two rooms, one at the lower level and one at the upper hall level.

Activities

■ 1. Do some research to learn more about Oxford Castle or some other English castle. Present the results of your research in a series of labeled pictures, floor plans, and diagrams.

▲ 2. Use modeling clay or some other similar substance to construct a round keep.

■ 3. Draw floor plans for the interior of a round keep.

★
■ 4. Although castles sound comfortable, romantic, and glamorous, in truth they were often cold, drafty, and sparsely furnished. Pretend that you are an architect or interior designer who has been hired by a wealthy lord to modernize and beautify his castle. Write a project proposal in which you analyze his structural and design problems and then explain in detail what changes you would recommend, what materials you would use, and what the anticipated costs would be. Write as if the times are medieval or modern, whichever you prefer, but be consistent. Once you have chosen a period, do not change.

Name _____

The Great Hall

The largest room in the keep was the **great hall**. This room was two stories high and of sufficient size to be used as a banquet hall, a living room, an office, and a playroom. In keeps without separate bedrooms, it also served as a dormitory.

The great hall was reached through doors that were set high above the ground. To enter, guests had to climb a ladder that could be raised in time of attack. Often the great hall was divided into two parts. One part, called the **solar**, faced the sun and was a more comfortable place to be. About twelve feet above the floor of the great hall ran a balcony that linked the family bedrooms. Below the great hall was a basement that served as both a storeroom and a dungeon.

By today's standards, most great halls were sparsely furnished. In the middle of the room were long wooden tables and benches where the people who worked at the castle sat during meals. At one end of the room was a raised platform, called a **dais**, on which the king and his family sat. Cupboards along the walls held dishes, and a huge fireplace supplied some warmth. The stone walls were decorated with banners and shields. In winter, great tapestries were hung over the stone to keep out the chill. The floor of the great hall was covered with reeds cut from a nearby riverbed. These reeds were warmer than the stone and concealed some of the garbage that was carelessly dropped during meals. Sometimes a spice called rosemary was sprinkled on the soiled reeds to freshen them. When there was more garbage than reeds, additional reeds were cut and spread over the top of the growing pile.

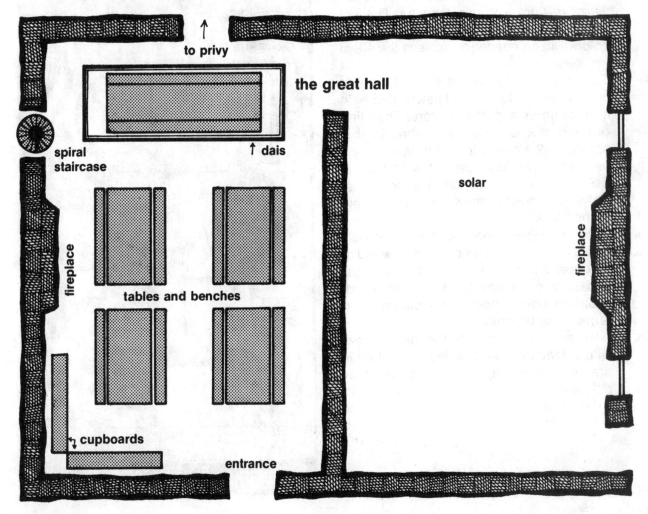

Name _____

The Great Hall
(continued)

Because the great hall had thick stone walls with only narrow slits to let in the sunlight, it was often dark and gloomy. But at night, in the glow of fire and candlelight, it became a festive place filled with acrobats, jesters, jugglers, minstrels, and musicians, who entertained the lord and his guests.

Outside the great hall, a narrow passageway led to a small room in which a wooden seat had been placed over a channel that ran through the wall and down the outside of the keep. This room was called a **garderobe**, or **privy**, and was the forerunner of today's bathroom.

Activities

1. Because the stone walls of castle keeps were often cold, damp, and drafty, heavy woven tapestries were hung over them during winter to keep out the chill. Do some research to learn more about tapestries. How and where were they made? What themes did they depict? Based on what you learn, design a simple tapestry. Draw a sketch of your design, and indicate what colors will be needed to achieve the effect you desire.

2. The dishes used in castles were often made of wood or pewter. Look at pewter dishes in a museum or department store. Then find out more about pewter. What is this substance? How is it made? Why was it used in the Middle Ages? Why is it still in use today? If possible, bring some pewter dishes to school to show to other members of the class.

3. Draw and label a floor plan for a great hall.

4. Using a wooden or cardboard box, wood or cardboard scraps, Popsicle sticks, sugar cubes, or other similar building materials, make an open model of a great hall, and furnish it appropriately.

5. Compare the great hall of medieval times with the family room of today. In what ways are they alike? In what ways are they different?

Name _____

A Day at the Castle

Most days at the castle followed a set routine. At dawn, the watchman sounded a horn from the battlements of the keep to announce the arrival of a new day. By five o'clock, everyone was up. Breakfast, served in the great hall, was little more than bread and ale. After this meal, everyone went to the chapel for Mass. When the church services were over, the work of the day began. The lord surveyed the manor. The women spent time sewing, weaving, and caring for the clothing. The servants went about their endless duties.

The midday meal was served between nine and eleven in the morning. Afterward, the lord heard and settled the bailiff's complaints about the peasants and meted out various punishments to the thieves and poachers among the villeins. He also inspected the work of the manor tenants and devoted some time to training his pages and knights.

The lady of the castle also had important work to do. She was responsible for overseeing the work of the household servants and for supervising the dairy, gardens, and kitchen. She had to make certain that the clothes-making industry of the fief continued, including the spinning, weaving, and sewing of cloth. It was her duty to train all of the girls and even the boys, until they were old enough to become pages and begin their training for knighthood. Sometimes, the lady of the manor embroidered cloth in bright colors and fancy stitches. When her busy schedule permitted, she read, wrote poems, or composed music. She also went riding and hunting with the lord of the manor and was expected to manage the estate in his absence.

Name _____

A Day at the Castle
(continued)

Often the evening meal at the castle was a great banquet. For the occasion, the lord, his lady, and their most important guests were seated at a table on the dais. People of less importance and castle servants were seated at other tables in the hall. Nobles were served with silver or pewter goblets and plates, while lesser guests drank from wooden goblets and ate from wooden platters called **trenchers**.

Following the meal, acrobats, dancers, jugglers, minstrels, and musicians entertained the lord and his guests. And, of course, there was always the fool. The fool, or **jester**, wore a costume that was half one color and half another, and he had a cap hung with bells. To make the guests laugh, he told crude jokes about the noble classes and did funny things.

Activities

● 1. In medieval times, salt was a very important commodity. It was used both to preserve foods and to flavor them. Kings and nobles had elaborate vessels called **saltcellars** in which the salt for table use was served. Look at pictures of saltcellars or visit a museum where actual saltcellars are on display.

■ 2. The English word **salary** comes from the
★ Latin word **salarius**, meaning "of or relating to salt." Do some research to learn the relationship between this seasoning and regular monetary compensation. With what were Roman soldiers paid? What does the phrase **worth your salt** mean?

■ 3. Write and present a short play depicting a day at a castle.

■ 4. Create a pantomime in which you are the jester at a castle and have been called to entertain important guests at a banquet.

■ 5. Compare a medieval banquet in a castle with a state dinner in the White House or a royal dinner in Buckingham Palace. In what ways are they similar? In what ways are they different?

Name _____

Foods of the Nobles

The diet of people during the Middle Ages was much simpler than our diet today. Because they had no refrigeration and little reliable transportation, they could eat only what they could raise or catch.

A variety of fruits, vegetables, and grains were grown on the manor grounds. The peasants planted carrots, lettuce, okra, onions, potatoes, spinach, and squash in the kitchen garden and harvested grapes from the castle vineyards and cherries, crab apples, nuts, and plums from manor orchards. In the fields, they raised barley, oats, rye, and wheat. The manor had its own mill where these grains were ground into flour for use in breads, cakes, and pastries.

The meat eaten in the great hall was raised in manor fields, caught in manor streams, or killed during hunts in manor forests. The lord and his guests ate salted beef, some fresh fish, and a variety of fowl, including chickens, partridges, peafowl, and pigeons. They also ate fresh pork, but it was tough and chewy because they did not know how to fatten their pigs properly.

To make these simple foods more interesting and palatable, people in medieval times seasoned them heavily with expensive imported spices. Because there was no sugar, honey was used as a sweetener, and each castle had its own beehives.

The lord and his guests drank water, milk, and wine, a usual manor favorite. They also consumed **verjuice**, a sour juice squeezed from crab apples or unripe grapes which resembles cider, and **mead**, a fermented drink made of water, honey, malt, and yeast.

Activities

★ 1. Pretend that your family has no refrigeration and that you cannot make frequent trips to a grocery store. Make a two-column chart. In one column, list all of the foods you eat and would still be able to enjoy if you had to raise and/or catch them yourself. In the other column, list the foods you now enjoy but would no longer be able to buy, keep, and eat under medieval conditions.

■ 2. Pretend that you are a publicist for a modern restaurant and amusement park built on a medieval theme. Guests at the park will walk over a drawbridge and enter through the portcullis. Meals will be served by costumed waiters and waitresses in a great hall. Prepare a menu for this restaurant. Then create a brochure in which you list and describe some of the other park attractions visitors might enjoy.

Name _____

Goblets and Trenchers

The foods eaten in the great hall were served on dishes made of a variety of materials. Their selection and use depended on the wealth of the castle lord and on the importance of his guests. For the lord, the members of his family, and their most important guests, there were goblets and plates made of gold, silver, or pewter. Less important guests and servants used wooden goblets and ate from wooden platters, called **trenchers**, which were often shared by two people. At this time, some people began to use forks, rather than their fingers, when they ate. Those who chose not to do so were required to dip their hands frequently into bowls of water so that their fingers would remain clean.

Servants at a castle banquet could tell what dishes to use for which guests by noting where these guests were seated with relation to the salt. Salt was very important in the medieval household. Kings and nobles had elaborately decorated containers called **saltcellars** in which salt for table use was stored and from which it was served. These containers were placed on the tables below royalty and the most important guests and above, or before, the tables of the less important guests. Those persons who sat "above the salt" ate from metal dishes that were filled with meat and vegetables. Those who sat "below the salt" ate from wooden trenchers and were seldom served meat. In fact, household servants of lower rank and villeins rarely ate meat.

Activities

■
★ 1. Make a chart showing common medieval
◉   foods. Arrange them by food group: meat, fish, poultry, and eggs; milk and cheese; fruits and vegetables; breads and cereals. Then, using what you know about nutrition, analyze the medieval diet to determine whether or not it was a balanced one. Summarize your findings in charts, graphs, and tables, and present them to the class in a brief oral report.

★
▬ 2. Do some research to learn what diseases and disabilities were common during the Middle Ages. Then analyze this disease-and-disability pattern to see if it is, in any way, diet related. Present your findings in comparable charts and graphs.

▲
▬ 3. Plan and prepare a medieval banquet. Make the atmosphere as much like that of a great hall as possible. Seat your guests at long tables, and provide jesters, jugglers, and other similar entertainment.

▬ 4. Compare the eating utensils used in medieval times with those in use today. In what ways are they alike? In what ways are they different? Present what you learn to the class by means of captioned and labeled charts, diagrams, and pictures.

Name _____

Medieval Dress

Despite the cold barrenness of the castles, most of them had splendidly carved chests full of exquisite clothing. Medieval clothes were made from a variety of fabrics. For everyday wear, there were linens, serges, worsteds, and felt. For more formal wear, there were brocades, silks, satins, taffetas, and velvets. Unlike Roman clothes, which were just wrapped around and tied, medieval clothes were cut and sewn to fit. They had necklines, bodices, sleeves, waists, and legs.

All clothing was not the same. Daytime clothes varied with the weather and with the tasks to be done. A young working man may have worn leather boots, stockings that reached his thighs and were attached to his underpants, a full-sleeved shirt or a tunic, a belt, and a cap.

The typical lord of a castle wore fine linen underwear, wool or silk stockings, and a white linen shirt or a tunic. For formal occasions, he would don a loose, sleeveless outer garment called a **mantle**, which was made of expensive imported fabric often woven with gold or silver threads and sometimes edged with a jeweled border or lined with squirrel fur.

Name _____

Medieval Dress
(continued)

Even in medieval times, women's fashions were influenced by French designs. Rich ladies wore dresses with fitted bodices, flowing skirts, and tight-fitting sleeves with more than fifty buttons on each arm. Their underclothing consisted of a long undergown and, under that, a short gown called a **chemise**. They also wore jackets, capes, and cloaks made of vibrant-colored fabrics and lined with ermine, an elegant white fur.

The most outstanding part of a medieval lady's costume was her headdress. One popular headdress was like a giant cornucopia, which had been inverted and was worn slanting up and back. From the high pointed end hung a veil that floated over the shoulders and down the back. This headdress was called a **barbette**. Another style of headdress was a **wimple**, a piece of silk or linen that was wrapped in layers around the head and over the chin, neck, and shoulders.

Activities

1. Make a collection of swatches of different kinds of fabrics that were used in the Middle Ages. Label each swatch.

2. Learn about the fibers that were available during the Middle Ages and the care they required. Which ones were the most popular? Why? How was clothing washed or cleaned?

3. Dress some dolls in medieval costumes.

4. Make a medieval headdress for yourself.

5. Compare the clothing worn in medieval times with that worn today. Tell which styles you would rather wear and why.

barbette

horned headdress

wimple

Name _____

Knighthood

Knighthood was an enviable rank that could not be inherited; it had to be learned and earned. Even the eldest son of a noble had to prove himself worthy of this rank, and only the sons of nobles and knights were allowed to enter training for it.

Knighthood training was begun when boys were only eight or nine years old. All of their games were planned to prepare them for a life of fighting. They practiced archery, fencing, and horsemanship in mock battles with other boys. They were not taught to read, to write, or to work math problems, because none of these skills was necessary to a fighter.

When a knight-in-training turned fifteen, he was sent away from home to the castle of a friend or relative to begin his formal training as a **page**. There, an older knight taught him battle techniques and the code of chivalrous behavior. He learned the customs of the tournament, and he learned to be gentle and polite. A knight was always supposed to behave like a gentleman.

At the age of eighteen, the youth became a **squire**. He was allowed to wear silver spurs and, for the first time, to go into combat with the knight to whom he was assigned. He served his master as a bodyguard and carried his master's armor and shield.

Castles, Codes, Calligraphy
© 1984 — The Learning Works, Inc.

Name _____

Knighthood
(continued)

When it was determined that a squire had learned his lessons well and was ready for knighthood, a simple ceremony was held in which he was **dubbed**, that is, officially made a knight. In preparation for this ceremony, the squire was bathed and then robed in white to symbolize the purity of his life as a knight. He knelt before his lord, who tapped him on each shoulder with the blade of his sword and said, "I dub thee knight." The former squire was now a **knight bachelor**.

The new knight received a variety of gifts. He was presented with a pair of golden spurs, which only knights could wear. He also received a new suit of armor, a sword, and a new shield emblazoned with his coat of arms. After the dubbing ceremony, he was the guest of honor at an elaborate banquet, which was held in the great hall to celebrate the occasion.

Activities

■ 1. Find out about various hand weapons used by knights. Then draw and label pictures of these weapons on a chart. Briefly describe how each one was used.

▲ 2. After a squire became a knight bachelor, there were other ranks of knighthood he could attain, depending on his abilities and wealth, ranks toward which knights worked throughout their lifetimes. Make a mobile showing the different ranks of knighthood.

■ 3. Design the shield you would use if you were made a knight.

■ 4. Write and stage a puppet show based on a dubbing ceremony.

Name _____

Chivalry

Chivalry was a code of conduct developed by the church and followed in medieval times by all men of high birth, especially nobles, knights, and kings. In the early days of feudalism, it included only loyalty and service. Later, when knighthood came to be looked upon as a gallant and romantic undertaking, bravery, honor, and generosity were added to the code. A knight was to defend the church, protect the weak, seek situations in which to exhibit his military skill, and be generous in his treatment of vanquished foes.

The code was not written down, but every knight knew it and passed it on to the pages and squires he trained. A knight was to be brave, modest, and pure in thought and conduct. He was to give to the poor, be gentle to the weak, defend the honor of women, and protect the very young and the very old. Above all, he was expected to act honorably in all situations and to keep his word.

Not all knights were chivalrous. Some of them chose to violate this code of conduct and to be, instead, bandits, robber barons, and thieves.

Activities

1. Chivalry is supposed to have reached its peak during the reign of King Arthur in England. Read about this monarch and his famous Knights of the Round Table in *Le Morte d'Arthur*, compiled and translated by Sir Thomas Malory.
2. Make a banner, poster, or embroidered sampler on which the rules of chivalry are written and illustrated.
3. Pantomime a series of situations selected to illustrate chivalrous behavior, and show what an ideal knight would do in each one.
4. **Knights-errant** were knights who traveled at random in search of opportunities to display their military prowess and generosity. Write a story about the adventures of a chivalrous knight-errant.

Name _____

Tournaments

Tournaments were the highlight of castle life. All manor residents and the inhabitants of neighboring castles were invited to attend. Visiting nobles were housed in the castle. Large, round, colorful tents were set up on the castle grounds for other guests. Wooden stands decorated with colorful awnings and pennants were erected for the spectators. Massive amounts of food were gathered and prepared for the huge banquets that accompanied the festivities.

A tournament usually consisted of only one event, the joust. The **joust** was a contest in which two knights on horseback galloped toward each other from opposite ends of a field, and each one tried to unseat the other with his lance. The knights were dressed in full armor and carried both lance and shield. They rode in narrow lanes separated only by a low fence. Each knight held his lance pointed forward and to the inside, toward his opponent. If a knight was knocked to the ground, he forfeited his armor and horse and had to pay a ransom to get them back. If three lances were splintered by two knights without either knight's being unhorsed, the contest was declared a draw. Even with only this one event, tournaments often lasted for days—until all of the knights had participated in the joust.

Activities

■ 1. Pretend that you are a modern-day network sports announcer and have been hired to broadcast a medieval joust. Write a script in which you set the scene for your listening or viewing audience and then describe the events as they take place. Include commercials for products that might have special appeal for your medieval audience.

■ 2. Compare the medieval joust and banquet with the more modern rodeo and barbecue. In what ways are they alike? In what ways are they different?

Name _____

Armor

    Armor is protective covering for the body which is worn in contests or in combat. Medieval armor was made of a wide variety of materials and in a wide variety of styles. Early armor consisted of a knee-length shirt or tunic, called a **hauberk**, which was worn with breeches. At first, hauberks were made of colored and stamped leather. Next, metal rings were sewn on the leather to keep a lance from penetrating it. Later, the small metal rings or scales were interlocked to make **mail**, and the leather was omitted altogether. Hauberks were then made entirely of a metal chain that consisted of as many as 250,000 links and took as long as four years to forge. Often a hood of mail was joined to the hauberk to protect the neck and the back of the head. Mail was relatively flexible. It was effective against swords and spears and could be easily rolled up for storage.

    As weapons changed, armor changed. When knights began to use the battle hammer and the battle-ax, better armor was needed. A blow from a battle-ax caused mail to cut into the flesh and created multiple wounds that were slow to heal. At first, metal plates were fastened onto the mail to cover the most vulnerable areas of the body. Eventually, plate armor replaced chain armor altogether and was used to cover the entire body.

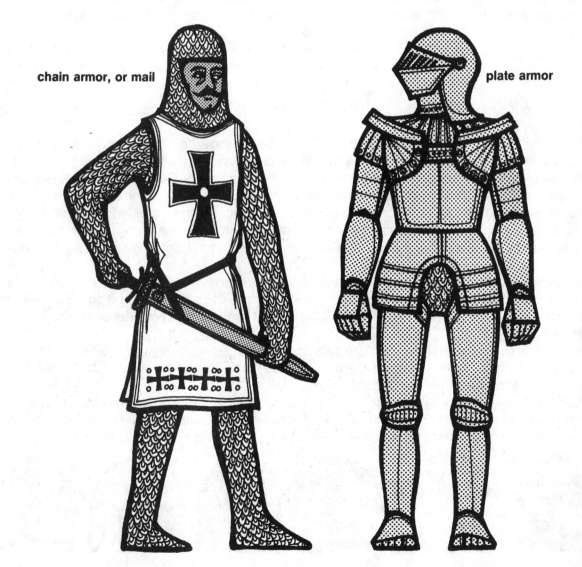

chain armor, or mail

plate armor

Armor
(continued)

Knights had their choice of several types of helmets. Some of these helmets had close-fitting hoods to cover the back of the head, some were cone-shaped with visors that could be lifted between battles, and some were kettle-shaped, covered the whole head, and had only slits for the eyes.

In contests or combat, nothing was left to chance. Even the knight's horse was well protected with armor, but plate armor was so cumbersome and clumsy that a knight often had to be hoisted into the saddle. Both knight and horse were totally helpless if they fell to the ground.

Except for slight variations in physical size and armor style, knights wearing armor looked very much alike. So that they could be readily identified as friend or foe, they often had pictures or symbols engraved on their helmet visors and on their armor breastplates. These engraved pictures were forerunners of the later coats of arms.

In addition to his armor, a knight often wore a richly ornamented sash or belt called a **baldric** over one shoulder, across his breast, and under the opposite arm to support his sword. He carried a shield large enough to be used as a litter if he was wounded and had to be carried from the field.

Eventually, armor was discarded. It had become too expensive to make, too clumsy to wear, and too ineffective to use against more modern weapons.

Activities

1. Read about armor. Collect and label pictures showing different kinds of armor. Share your collection with the class.

2. Sew small metal rings or plates to stiff cloth or leather to show how early hauberks were made.

3. Apparently, the Roman soldiers wore armor made of leather and metal. Trace the styles of armor and other forms of protection used by soldiers throughout history. Compare these with the types of weapons developed. Note how each one has changed in response to the other. More effective weapons have required more protective armor which has, in turn, created the need for even more destructive weapons. This phenomenon might be termed the "armor and arms race."

4. Write a story or fable about the plight of a knight who, with his horse, has fallen and is literally pinned beneath his armor.

5. Do some research to learn the correct names for the different parts or pieces of chain or plate armor. Then design an ideal suit of armor. Label the parts of your design and post it as part of a class display entitled **What the Well-Dressed Knight Is Wearing This Season** or **Knight-Time Wear**.

6. In columns of a table, list the advantages and disadvantages of armor made from mail and armor made from metal plates. Compare the two, then design a medieval suit of armor in which you incorporate the best features of each.

7. Astronauts wear specially designed suits to protect them in a hostile environment. Compare a medieval suit of armor with a modern spacesuit. In what ways are they alike? In what ways are they different? Consider purpose, shape, features, and function.

Name _____

Weapons

A number of different weapons were used to attack a castle. These weapons were designed primarily to penetrate armor and walls and to throw arrows, fireballs, or stones.

One of the weapons used for throwing was a **crossbow**. It consisted of a bow set on a stock. Its advantage was that it was much more powerful than a conventional bow and could be used to fire stones and metal, as well as darts and arrows. Its chief disadvantage was that it was stiff and took a long time to operate. To cock a crossbow, the archer stood it up on the stock, placed one foot in the stirrup, and used a special belt claw or pulley to draw the bowstring up and over a notched piece connected to the trigger. When the archer released the trigger, the crossbow fired a short, flat, blunt-headed arrow, called a **bolt** or **quarrel**, with tremendous force.

Two other weapons used for throwing were the catapult and the ballista. The **catapult** was like a giant slingshot and was used to hurl javelin-like shafts. The **ballista**, a giant crossbow on a platform, was used to throw stones and balls of fire. It was cocked by using a crank, called a **windlass**, to twist and thus increase the tension on a skein of rope or cord. This rope or cord was attached to the arm of the ballista. When the tension on this cord was suddenly released, the arm flew forward, hurling its destructive projectile.

Among the larger weapons were several mechanical devices designed to knock down doors and to drill holes in walls. The **battering ram** consisted of a huge tree trunk with a head of iron. Hung by chains from a tower, it was pulled back and then released so that it would swing forward and beat down the castle walls. The **bore** was also a tree trunk but different from the battering ram in that it was pointed on one end and was used for opening a hole in the wall rather than for knocking it down.

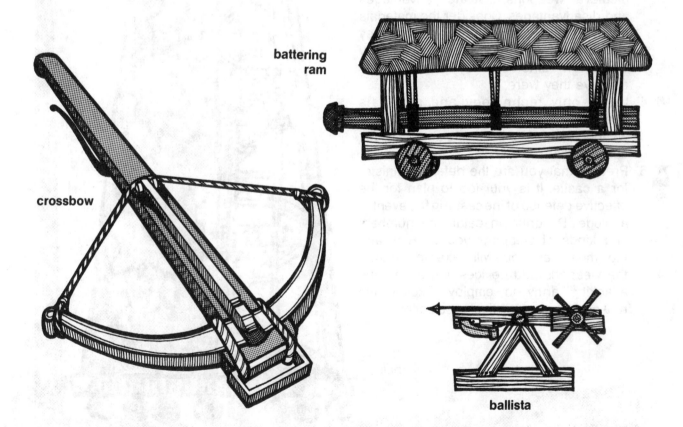

battering ram

crossbow

ballista

Name _____

Weapons
(continued)

To defend the castle, knights stood on the battlements and shot down at their attackers. The attackers, in turn, used a movable roofed shelter called a **cat** to protect them from these defenders' arrows. This shelter was shaped like a long, narrow shed. It had walls along the sides but was open at both ends. Its roof was covered with iron and raw hides and sloped sharply so that stones and arrows would fall off.

When nothing else worked, attacking armies built a movable war tower, called a **belfry**. This tower consisted of a wooden ladder and scaffolding, covered with wet hides to protect it from fire. It was rolled on logs to a position near the castle. Then soldiers climbed to the top of the tower, dropped a drawbridge over the castle parapet, and jumped from it onto the castle grounds.

Activities

1. Do some research to learn more about one of these weapons. Then write and illustrate a detailed description of its construction and its use.

2. Make a working model of one of these weapons or devices.

3. Analyze and evaluate several of these medieval weapons. List their advantages and disadvantages. Consider the materials of which they were made, how heavy they were, how movable and maneuverable they were, how vulnerable they were, and how effective they were.

4. Using only technology and materials available in medieval times, design a weapon that would penetrate armor and/or castle walls.

5. Pretend that you are the defense minister for a castle. It is your job to plan for the effective defense of the castle in the event of a siege. Describe in detail the numbers and kinds of weapons you will use and the measures you will take to counter the weapons and devices you expect the attacking army to employ. Explain the reasons for your particular selections.

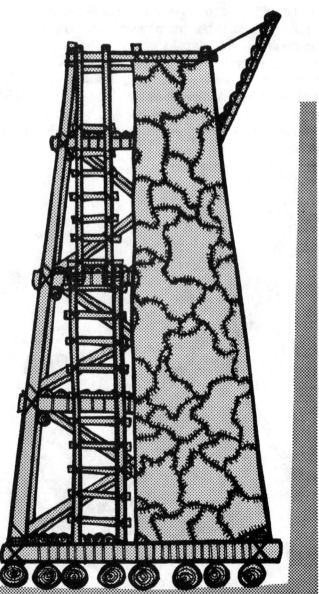

belfry

Name _____

The Siege

Various battle tactics were used during the siege of a castle. Sometimes, to cross a deep moat, the attacking soldiers filled it with bundles of brush and sticks. Then they simply walked across. They were protected while they worked by a movable shelter with a sloping roof that resembled a **cat** but was called a **penthouse**.

Sometimes, the attackers dug a tunnel under the foundations of the castle, reinforcing the tunnel walls with wooden timbers as they went. Occasionally, they were able to use a tunnel of this type to gain access to the castle grounds, but more often they simply burned the supporting timbers once the tunnel was completed, thus leaving the wall or building above inadequately supported and causing it to collapse.

Great preparations were made by both sides before a siege. After everyone who lived near the castle moved inside, the portcullis was lowered, and the drawbridge was raised and bolted into place. Within the castle, firewood and caldrons were carried to the roof, fires were lighted, and water and tar were heated to pour down on anyone who tried to scale the walls. At the same time, the attackers readied their machines and donned their suits of armor. Next, they mounted several kinds of attacks in an attempt to make an opening, or **breach**, in the castle wall so that they could swarm in.

Name _____

The Siege
(continued)

Inside the castle, the defenders not only tried to keep their attackers from putting a hole in the wall, but they also attempted to kill or wound as many of the enemy as possible. The **arrow slits** in castle walls allowed these archers more opportunities to shoot without making targets of themselves.

Activities

■ 1. According to mythology, the Greeks used a trick to get inside the walls of Troy during the Trojan War. Troy, an ancient city, was a walled combination of fort, palace, and warehouse, not unlike a medieval castle. Although the Trojan army was much less powerful than the attacking Greek army, Troy was well fortified, and the Greeks could not gain entry. The siege lasted ten years. Finally, the Greeks built a hollow wooden horse. Some Greek soldiers hid inside, and the others abandoned their camp. The unsuspecting Trojans dragged the horse into their city. That night, while the Trojan soldiers slept, the Greek soldiers climbed out of the horse and opened the city gates, letting in the rest of the Greek army. Read about the Trojan War and about the Trojan horse.

■ 2. Think up and describe a trick similar to the Greek one that might be used to get inside a well-fortified medieval castle.

★ 3. The Trojan War is supposed to have lasted for ten long years. List and describe some of the problems that might arise if a siege lasted that long. How would the people inside the castle obtain sufficient supplies of food and water? Where would the attacking army get its supplies? What might happen if one army or the other ran out of food, water, or weapons?

Name _____

The Protection of a Castle

Because early castles were made largely of wood (see page 15), the biggest threat to them was fire. The main way to protect these castles from fire was to soak animal hides with water and then to lay these hides over the wooden structures, such as the palisade and the tower. Protection of this sort was temporary because the hides soon dried out.

A more permanent way to protect against fire was to build with stone instead of wood. The moat-and-bailey castles with walls and keeps of stone were far less likely to be set afire during a siege.

Another way of protecting a castle was to design it so that it would be difficult to attack. Some castles were built on cliffs or hills so that they would be hard to reach. Many castles had moats and walls around them, and some even had more than one moat. The idea was to put many natural and artificial barriers in the way of an attacking army so that few enemy soldiers could get through to storm the castle.

Yet another way of protecting a castle was to design it so that it would be easy to defend. Later castles had **battlements**, or walls with high places to hide behind and low places to look and shoot through. The high places were called **merlons**, and the low places were called **crenels**, or **embrasures**. For many years, attacking armies simply could not penetrate a castle built in this way.

Activities

1. Draw up a plan of attack for an army to follow in laying siege to a castle. Describe how the members of this army will defend themselves against arrows shot from the battlements above and how they will gain entry to the castle.

2. Tell which side—the attackers or the defenders—you think usually won a siege and why.

Name _____

Posttest

Write the correct answer on each line.

1. The wooden fence that surrounded the tower of an early castle was called a _____ .

2. The ditch around a castle was called a _____ .

3. The main room of the castle keep, or tower, was the _____ .

4. The raised platform where the lord of the manor sat during meals was called a _____ .

5. Visitors of lesser importance sat below the _____ .

6. Before becoming a knight, a boy had to spend at least three years as a _____ .

7. For protection in competition and combat, a knight wore a suit of _____ .

8. Two knights competed against each other in a _____ .

9. The knight's unwritten code of honorable behavior was _____ .

10. The castle entertainer, or "fool," was also called the _____ .

Write **T** in front of each statement that is true. Write **F** in front of each statement that is false.

_____ 11. Roman castles were made of dirt.

_____ 12. Kings often had many castles.

_____ 13. There was no way for a villein to leave a manor.

_____ 14. During a siege, the attackers were sometimes protected by a cat.

_____ 15. The strong entrance gate to a castle was called a portcullis.

_____ 16. The wimple and the barbette were types of armor.

_____ 17. Medieval clothing was made from a variety of fabrics and, unlike Roman clothing, was cut and sewn to fit.

_____ 18. Castles were elaborately decorated and immaculately clean.

_____ 19. In medieval times, pewter was used to make plates and goblets.

_____ 20. The diet of people during the Middle Ages was much simpler than our diet today.

Correlated Activities

● 1. Visit a museum and take special note of costumes worn, dishes used, books written, tapestries woven, and other art produced during the Middle Ages.

■ 2. Tell how chivalry was exemplified in the stories about King Arthur and his Knights of the Round Table.

◼ 3. Pretend that you are a page in service at a lord's castle. Write a letter home describing your experiences.

◼ 4. Pretend that you are the lord or lady of a castle. Write a diary account of one day's activities.

Answer Key

Pretest				Posttest			
1.	A	11.	G	1.	palisade	11.	T
2.	S	12.	H	2.	moat	12.	T
3.	I	13.	K	3.	great hall	13.	F
4.	M	14.	Q	4.	dais	14.	T
5.	T	15.	J	5.	salt	15.	T
6.	F	16.	C	6.	page	16.	F
7.	B	17.	R	7.	armor	17.	T
8.	L	18.	N	8.	joust	18.	F
9.	E	19.	O	9.	chivalry	19.	T
10.	P	20.	D	10.	jester	20.	T

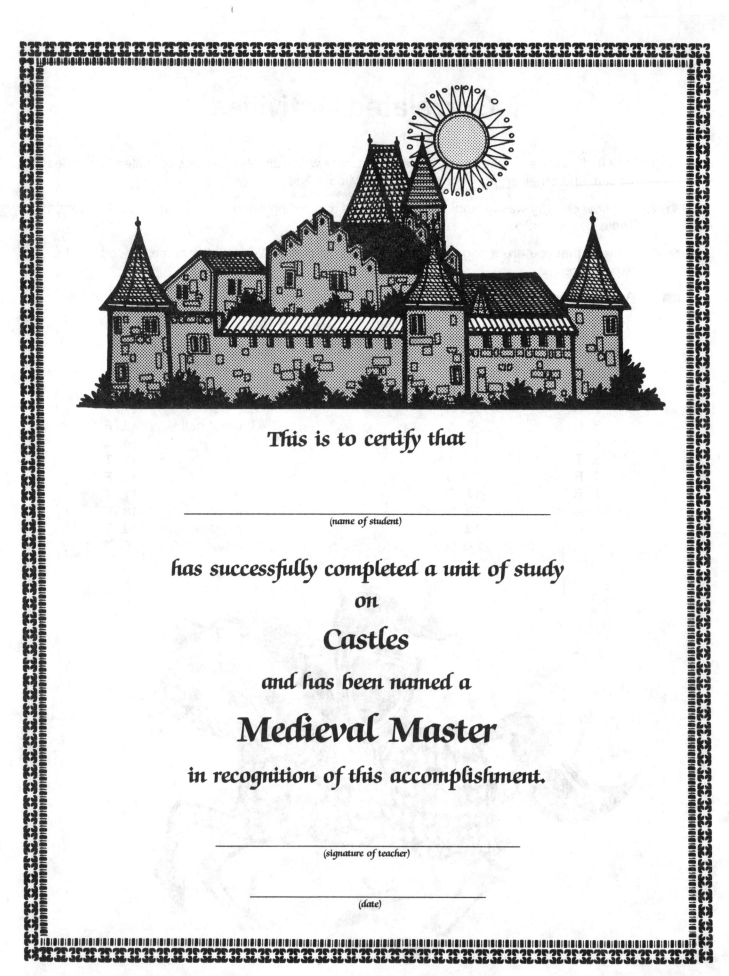

This is to certify that

_____
(name of student)

has successfully completed a unit of study

on

Castles

and has been named a

Medieval Master

in recognition of this accomplishment.

_____
(signature of teacher)

_____
(date)

Bulletin Board Ideas

Be a Secret Spy!

BREAK THE CODE

Can you break the code and solve these mysteries?

Take one

ADD A CIPHER

phone-a-code

paper clip code

rail fence code

tick-tack-toe code

shift codes

computer card code

shopping list codes

Learning Center Ideas

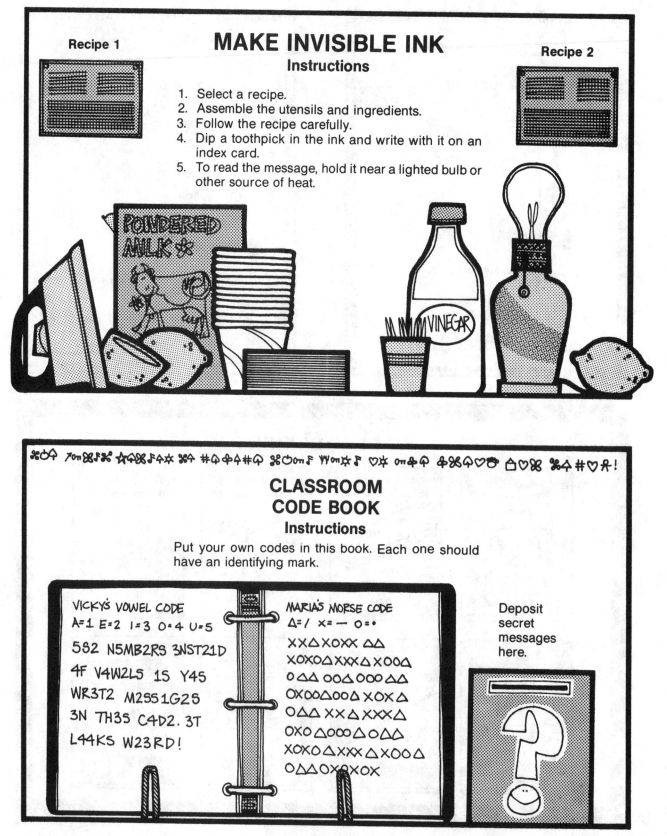

Recipe 1

MAKE INVISIBLE INK
Instructions

1. Select a recipe.
2. Assemble the utensils and ingredients.
3. Follow the recipe carefully.
4. Dip a toothpick in the ink and write with it on an index card.
5. To read the message, hold it near a lighted bulb or other source of heat.

Recipe 2

CLASSROOM CODE BOOK
Instructions

Put your own codes in this book. Each one should have an identifying mark.

VICKY'S VOWEL CODE
A=1 E=2 I=3 O=4 U=5

5S2 N5MB2RS 3NST21D
4F V4W2LS 1S Y45
WR3T2 M2SS1G2S
3N TH3S C4D2. 3T
L44KS W23RD!

MARIA'S MORSE CODE
∆=/ x=— o=•

XX∆ XOXX ∆∆
XOXO∆XXX∆XOO∆
O∆∆ OO∆ OOO ∆∆
OXOO∆OO∆ XOX∆
O∆∆ XX∆ XXX∆
OXO ∆OOO∆O∆∆
XOXO∆XXX∆XOO∆
O∆∆OXOXOX

Deposit secret messages here.

Codes

Name _____

Pretest

Match the following words with their definitions by writing the correct letter on each line.

_____ 1. cipher

_____ 2. code

_____ 3. cryptographer

_____ 4. cryptography

_____ 5. decode

_____ 6. encode

_____ 7. null letters

_____ 8. shift code

_____ 9. template

_____ 10. St. Cyr slide

A. a slotted device used to hide brief messages within longer texts and to find messages that have been hidden in this way

B. a code devised by moving letters in alphabetical order a certain number of spaces

C. a device used to encipher and decipher messages written in a shift code

D. a method of systematically changing a written text to conceal its meaning by substituting new letters for existing ones

E. the science or practice of enciphering and deciphering messages written in secret code

F. letters that are not part of a message but are inserted when the message is encoded to fill spaces and/or to mislead unauthorized readers

G. a person who specializes in enciphering and deciphering secret messages

H. to translate the symbols in which a message has been written into a form that is more easily understood

I. to write a message entirely in symbols

J. a system of symbols—letters, numbers, pictures, or words—that are assigned special meaning and are used to communicate

Ciphers are one type of code. Read the names of the codes listed below. Underline the ones that are true ciphers.

11. Caesar's code

12. columns of four

13. keyword match code

14. Morse code

15. phone-a-code

16. symbolic code

17. tick-tack-toe code

18. triple threat code

Decipher the following messages.

19. ·—— /·—··/·/—/···/·//—·—·/———/——/·//····/———/——/·//·—··—·—

_____

20. Ⅴ□Ⅴ□ ⅗⅌ ⅂Ⅿ□ □⅃⅃⅂Ⅴ⅂Ⅿ□⅍

_____

⅃⅌ <⅌□ >⅌⅍Ⅴ Ⅴ⅍< ⅂Ⅿ⅂□ ⅂□ □⅃<<□⅃ ⅃⅂⅂□□⅃ □⅍⅃□?

Castles, Codes, Calligraphy
© 1984 — The Learning Works, Inc.

43

Name _____

Codes and Ciphers

A **code** is a system of symbols—letters, numbers, pictures, or words—that are assigned special meanings and are used to communicate messages. **Cipher** is one kind of code. It is a method of systematically changing a written text to conceal its meaning by substituting new letters for existing ones. In other kinds of codes, words may be substituted for words. For example, the word *yellow* may stand for *danger.*

When you want to send a message in code, you must put your words into code or cipher form. You must **encode** or **encipher** your message. When you receive a message written in a code with which you are familiar, you must **decipher** it, or figure it out. When you receive a message written in a code with which you are unfamiliar, you must **crack**, or **break**, the code before you can begin to decipher the message. The process of enciphering and deciphering messages written in secret code is called **cryptography**, and specialists in this field are called **cryptographers**.

Ciphers and codes have been around since the dawn of recorded history. The Greeks used shorthand ciphers. During the last century B.C., Caesar and Cicero used codes in ancient Rome while Cleopatra was developing her secret ciphers in Egypt. In the Middle Ages, people sometimes used invisible inks to conceal their written messages from prying eyes.

Secret messages were frequently sent during the Renaissance. Even royalty used codes. When Mary, Queen of Scots, was imprisoned in England, she exchanged letters with Anthony Babington, a conspirator who was trying to murder Queen Elizabeth I and release Mary. Of course, Mary encouraged him. Meanwhile, Francis Walsingham, Elizabeth's secretary of state, had set up an organized and efficient system of secret intelligence to detect plots against the English queen. Unfortunately for Mary, her letters fell into the hands of Walsingham's spies. Even more unfortunately, the code in which Mary had written her letters was all too easily deciphered. Charged with being an accomplice in Babington's plot, Mary was tried and found guilty, largely on the basis of her own letters. On February 8, 1587, she was beheaded.

Activities

■ 1. Until the sixteenth century, there was not much need for codes, because so few people could read or write. Writing, itself, was a kind of "code," because so few people could understand written messages. Do some research to discover the ways in which people sent messages *before* they could read or write. Share what you learn with the class by means of a chart or poster.

▲ 2. Use one of the communication methods you
◉   read about in activity 1 to send a message to a friend. Then evaluate your results. How successful were you at sending the message? How successful was your friend at receiving and understanding the message? Did he or she get only the general idea or understand *exactly* what you had said?

Name _____

Mirror Writing

One of the easiest codes to encipher and to decipher is mirror writing. Most people print their mirror messages; but some handwrite them, which makes them a bit more difficult to decipher. To decipher a message written in mirror writing, simply hold it up to a mirror and read.

Activities

▲ 1. Copy your spelling list in mirror writing.
▲ 2. Make up a math worksheet for your class. Print the instructions in mirror writing.
▲ 3. Create a treasure map. Use mirror writing to write place-names on the map.

Metric Rule Code

The metric rule code is simple, also. First, place a metric ruler on your paper, and write one letter of your message above each of the centimeter markings. Next, put a box around the final letter of your message. Finally, fill in the spaces with other letters to mislead any unauthorized readers.

Activities

▲ 1. Use the metric rule code to write a short message to a friend.
■ 2. Devise a code similar to the metric rule code, but use a different measurement tool.

W E / W I L L / B E / T H E R E / A T / S E V E N

OWRESWRILL BLABEELTSHOEPRIEDARTOSTERVEER[N]OSLINGYZMPO

Columns of Four

Columns of four is a difficult code to break. When you use this code, encoding is a three-part process. First, write out your message and divide it into groups of four letters. If any group is short a letter or letters, fill in with null, or misleading, letters. Second, print the letters vertically in columns of four. Third, recopy the letters as they appear horizontally.

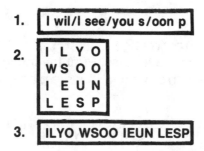

Of course, you can vary this code by using columns of three or five, or by writing the words as they appear diagonally.

Decipher these messages.

1. WGEYN HRAOY AARUS TDEIT

_____

2. MAHHO ANAEK RNSBS IETOP

_____

Encipher these messages.

3. Go to bed early.

_____

4. Watch TV today at four.

_____

Activities

▲ 1. Use this code to arrange a secret meeting with a friend. See if the friend actually meets you.
▲ 2. Design two variations on this code.
▲ 3. Make up a code that reads diagonally, and print instructions for using it.

Name _____

Shopping List Codes

A code is less likely to be broken if it is hidden so that no one even realizes that it is a code. One good way to do so is by using a shopping list. In this shopping list, the number amount is used to indicate which letter should be read. Ignore all quantity labels, such as *doz., lbs., pkg., boxes,* and the like.

Encoded Message	Decoded Message
3 cat food 2 dog biscuits 6 frozen vegetables 1 ice cream 2 doz. eggs 1 ham 2 steaks	TONIGHT

This second shopping list is a variation on the first one. Instead of looking at the number in front of each item, you look only at the first number in the list. It indicates the letter position for all of the entries that follow.

Encoded Message	Decoded Message
2 bags shell macaroni 5 lemons 1 pkg. blueberries 1 can flea powder 6 ears corn	HELLO

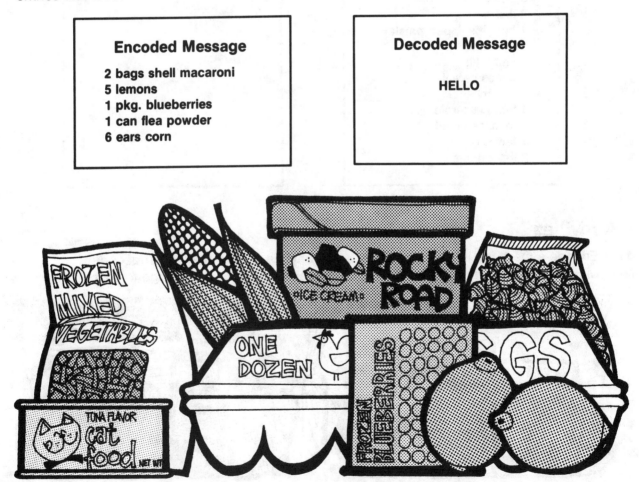

Name _____

Shopping List Codes
(continued)

Decipher these codes.

1.

Encoded Message
6 jars berry jam
2 bags corn
1 doz. eggs
1 ham
4 loaves bread
6 rolls towels
1 carton ice cream
4 tubes toothpaste

Decoded Message

2.

Encoded Message
2 bottles shoe polish
8 pears
2 lbs. tripe
1 bunch snipped parsley
1 lb. bacon
1 umbrella
3 boxes cereal
2 gal. milk
1 head escarole
1 lb. sliced beef
1 bottle lye
2 lbs. onions

Decoded Message

Activities

▲1. Encode a message in a shopping list. See if anyone in your family can decode it.

▲2. Make up a school supplies shopping list containing a special message to your teacher.

Name _____

Caesar's Code

Julius Caesar was a Roman general and politician who lived between 100 B.C. and 44 B.C. He was as clever as he was famous and is known to have used ciphers during his military career. Some of the codes he used were very complex, but the code we associate with him is one of the easiest codes to use. It is called a **shift code** because all of the letters are written in order and then shifted a certain number of places, or letters, forward, or to the right. If the letters are shifted one letter, *A* becomes *B*, *B* becomes *C*, and so on. In Caesar's code, the shift is three letters so that *A* becomes *D*, *B* becomes *E*, and so on to the end of the alphabet.

| A B C D E F G H I J K L M N O P Q R S T U V W X Y Z | plain |

| D E F G H I J K L M N O P Q R S T U V W X Y Z A B C | cipher |

One way to set up a shift code is by using a **St. Cyr slide**. This encoding device is a card with the alphabet printed on it. It has double sets of slits at each end through which a long strip of paper with the alphabet printed on it twice can be pulled. This strip is moved so that the letters on it align with the stationary letters on the card. In this way, a code is devised.

| | A B C D E F G H I J K L M N O P Q R S T U V W X Y Z | |
| A B C | E F G H I J K L M N O P Q R S T U V W X Y Z A B C D | F G H |

Once you have devised your code by shifting the letters, you can further confuse anyone who might try to break your code by dividing the message into four- or five-letter groups.

Decipher the following messages.

1. YMNX NXFA FWNF YNTS TKHF JXFW XHTI J   (**Clue**: The shift is 5.)

_____

2. IWXH RDST WPHP HWXU IDUU XUIT TC

_____

Activity

▲ Pretend that you are a classroom cryptographer. Put into code a message for a friend in another classroom.

Name _____

Key Word Match Code

A key word match code is a shift code in which a key word is used to determine the amount of the letter shift. This code differs from Caesar's code in that the shift is separately determined for each letter of the message.

To set up a key word match code, select a key word (for example, **school**) and write it above the message you wish to encode, repeating it as many times as are necessary.

SC HOOL SCHO   key word

WE NEED HELP   message

Then, use a St. Cyr slide to encode the message. To find what letter will be used in place of *W*, align the letter *S* on the slide with the letter *A* on the card. When you do so, you will discover that there has been a shift of eighteen and that *O* now stands for *W*.

| A B C D E F G H I J K L M N O P Q R S T U V W X Y Z |
| Q | S T U V W X Y Z A B C D E F G H I J K L M N O P Q R | T U |

Next, align the letter *C* on the St. Cyr slide with the letter *A* to determine what letter will be used in place of *E*. When you do so, you will discover that there has been a shift of two and that *G* now stands for *E*.

| A B C D E F G H I J K L M N O P Q R S T U V W X Y Z |
| A | C D E F G H I J K L M N O P Q R S T U V W X Y Z A B | D E |

Continue in this manner until the message is entirely encoded.

OG USSO ZGSD   encoded message

Name _____

Key Word Match Code
(continued)

Using **school** as the key word, decipher the following messages.

1. ZCWDM YWY FSOC

_____

2. LJL RCR AU HGZPWR

_____

Again using **school** as the key word, encipher the following messages.

3. Her mother made a quilt.

_____

4. The papers blew away.

_____

Activities

■ 1. Draw and label a poster or chart showing how to make and use a St. Cyr slide.

▲ 2. Using cardboard, tagboard, wood, or plastic, create a large St. Cyr slide for use by the cryptographers in your classroom.

★ 3. Analyze the key word match code. How **efficient** is it? How long does it take to encode a short message in key word match code? How **effective** is it? How difficult is it to decode a message that has been written in key word match code if you do *not* know the key word? What happens to the letter patterns that are usually used as decoding clues when each letter is encoded separately in this manner? How **reliable** is this code? What is the likelihood that there will be encoding and/or decoding errors?

■ 4. Compare Caesar's code with the key word match code. In what ways are these two codes alike? In what ways are they different? Which one is the most difficult to encipher? Which one is the most difficult to decipher?

◉ 5. If you had a secret message to send, would you use Caesar's code or the key word match code? Why?

Codes

Name _____

Rail Fence Code

The rail fence code is an old code but a good one. To encipher a message in this code, first write the words of the message in two rows so that the letters are staggered. Next, compress the letters in the first row. Then, compress the letters in the second row and write them beside the letters in the first row. Finally, divide this single row of letters into groups of four letters and use null letters to fill in any spaces in the final letter group. For additional confusion, place a null letter at the beginning of the message, *before* you divide the letters into four-letter groups.

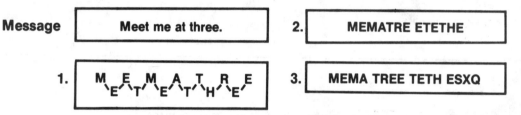

Message — Meet me at three.

2. MEMATRE ETETHE

1. M E M A T R E / E T E T H E

3. MEMA TREE TETH ESXQ

1. Decipher this message: WHVA USIU EOAD EAES BTTT TDYZ

_____

2. Encipher this message: Sue got an A on her test.

_____

Activities

▲ 1. Write a message in rail fence code to your teacher. See if he or she can decipher it.

■ 2. Compare the columns of four code with the rail fence code. In what ways are these two codes alike? In what ways are they different?

Name _____

Name It Code

When using the name it code, you hide your message in the initials within a list of names.

<table>
<tr><td>

Encoded Message

Sam <u>G</u>. Hopper
Mr. <u>O</u>. <u>H</u>. Simpson
Phil <u>O</u>. Hughes
Jane <u>M</u>. Henry
Alice <u>E</u>. Clinton

</td><td>

Decoded Message

GO HOME

</td></tr>
</table>

1. Decipher this message.

<table>
<tr><td>

Encoded Message

Sue H. Meyer
Brent E. Allen
Louise L. Joyce
Cary P. Box

</td><td>

Decoded Message

</td></tr>
</table>

2. Encipher this message: Wear a rose.

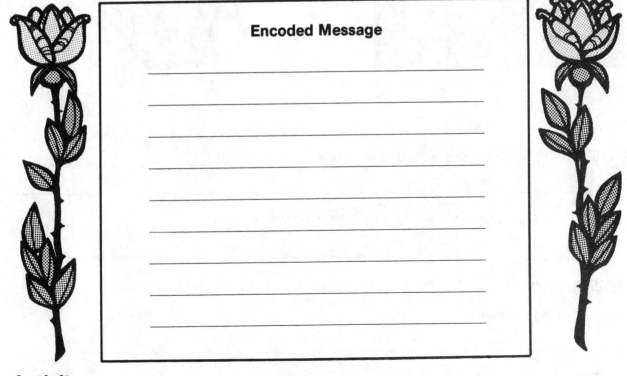

Encoded Message

_____

_____

_____

_____

_____

_____

_____

_____

Activity

▲ List the full names of all of the students in your class. Use this list to write a message in name it code.

Name _____

Phone-a-Code

Phone buttons can be used to create a code. They have all of the letters except *Q* and *Z*. To solve this problem, let 1 be *Q* and 0 be *Z*. Because each button has three letters on it, you will need a way to distinguish among the letters in each group of three. If the letter is on the left-hand side, place a dot to the left of the corresponding button number. If the letter is on the right-hand side, place a dot to the right of the number. If the letter is in the middle, no dot is needed. Thus, •2 is *A*, 2 is *B*, and 2• is *C*.

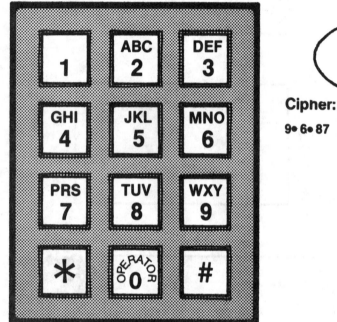

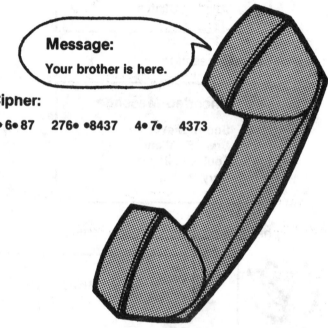

Message:

Your brother is here.

Cipher:

9• 6• 87   276• •8437   4• 7•   4373

Decipher these messages.

1. 8 7• 3   •8 4 3   •7 4 6• 6 3   2 8 •8 •8 6• 6 7•

    _____

2. 4• 5• 4• 5 3   4 6• 7 7• 3 7•   •2 6 •3   •3 6• •4 7•

    _____

Encipher these messages.

3. Fred has your pencil.

    _____

4. Derek is sick today.

    _____

Name _____

Tick-Tack-Toe Code

Tick-tack-toe code is an old code. It was used by the Confederate Army during the Civil War and has many variations. It is based on the positions of letters within a matrix and within the spaces formed by an X. In this code, each letter is represented by the lines that define the space that letter occupies. For example, ⌐ is *A*, ⊔ is *B*, and ⌐ is *C*. Tick-tack-toe code is also called **pigpen code** because of the "fences" between the letters.

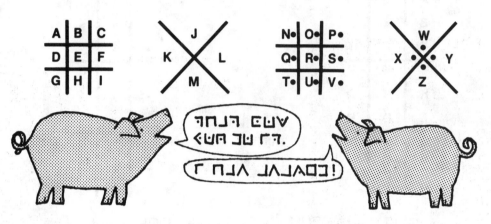

Encoded message: ⌐⌐⊔⌐⊔ ⌐⊔⊔⊔⌐⊔⌐ ⊐⌐⌐.

Decoded message: Caesar conquered Gaul.

Decipher these messages.

1. ⌐⊔< ⊓⌐⊔⌐ ⊐⌐⊔⊔⌐⊔⌐⌐ ⊐⌐⊔⌐⊔.

_____

2. ⊔⊐⌐⊔⌐⊔⌐⊔ ⊔⊐ ⊔⌐⊔ ⌐⌐⊔⌐ ⊔⊔⌐⌐⊔⌐⌐.

_____

Encipher these messages.

3. Jefferson bought the Louisiana Purchase.

_____

4. California has many missions.

_____

Activities

● 1. Do some research to learn how the Confederate Army used this code. Share what you learn with the class.

■ 2. Make a poster or chart on which you explain how to use this code.

▲ 3. Design two variations of the tick-tack-toe code.

Name _____

Triple Threat Code

Triple threat code is a variation of tick-tack-toe code. In triple threat, each letter is represented by the lines that define the space in which that letter appears and by a dot that indicates the position of that letter within the space. The dot can be in one of three positions—high, middle, or low. For example, ⌐ is A, ⌐ is B, and ⌐ is C.

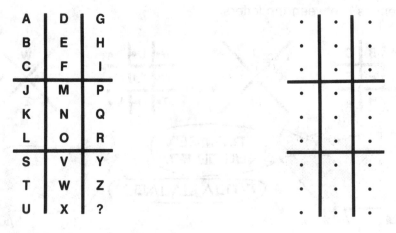

Encoded message: ⌐⌐⌐⌐ ⌐⌐⌐⌐⌐⌐⌐⌐ ⌐⌐⌐ ⌐⌐⌐⌐⌐⌐⌐⌐⌐

Decoded message: Bell invented the telephone.

Decipher these messages.

1. ⌐⌐⌐ ⌐⌐⌐⌐ ⌐⌐⌐ ⌐⌐ ⌐⌐⌐⌐⌐⌐⌐⌐

_____

2. ⌐⌐⌐⌐⌐⌐ ⌐⌐⌐⌐⌐⌐ ⌐⌐ ⌐⌐⌐⌐ ⌐⌐⌐⌐⌐⌐

_____

Encipher these messages.

3. Jeff has a new lunch pail.

_____

4. The typewriter is broken.

_____

Activities

▲ 1. Use graph paper to write a message in triple threat code.

■ 2. Compare triple threat code with tick-tack-toe code. In what ways are these two codes alike? In what ways are they different?

◉ 3. Evaluate triple threat code and tick-tack-toe code. Decide which one would be easier to learn and use. Tell which one would be harder to crack and why. Explain which one you would choose if you had a secret message to send.

Crossword Clues Code

When you use crossword clues code, the finished coded message looks just like a crossword puzzle. To decipher the code, you must read horizontally, one line at a time, and look at each letter that comes immediately *after* a blackened square. Variations would be to read vertically or to look at each letter that comes immediately *before* a blackened square.

Encoded Message

Decoded Message

I WILL SEE YOU
LATER.

Decipher the following message.

Encoded Message

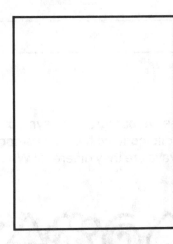

Decoded Message

Activities

● 1. Draw a master grid on clear plastic to help you when you use this method of coding.

▲ 2. Write a message in a crossword clues code which must be read *vertically,* rather than horizontally.

■ 3. Create a crossword puzzle for members of your class to work. Hide a secret message in it.

Name _____

Symbolic Code

A symbolic code is one in which a random symbol is used to stand for each letter of the alphabet. As you might imagine, this randomness makes symbolic codes difficult to decipher.

A B C D E F G H I J K L M

N O P Q R S T U V W X Y Z

Decode this message.

1.

_____

Encode this message.

2. I like vacations.

_____

Write a message in symbolic code on the upper line. Then ask a friend to decode this message and write it in words on the lower line.

3. _____

_____

Activities

▲ 1. Write an informative paragraph in symbolic code.

■ 2. Compare symbolic code with Caesar's code (see page 49). In what ways are these two codes alike? In what ways are they different? Which one would probably be more difficult to decipher? Why?

Name _____

Typewriter Code

Typewriter code is one kind of symbolic code. In typewriter code, letters are typed in alphabetical order directly from a typewriter keyboard, and then they are matched with symbols or numbers from the same keyboard to create a code.

A	B	C	D	E	F	G	H	I	J	K	L	M
"	#	$	%	?	&	/	(	)	*	+	2	3

N	O	P	Q	R	S	T	U	V	W	X	Y	Z
4	5	6	7	8	9	0	—	=	@	¢	§	!

Decode this message.

1. 2 ? 0 9   / 5   0 5   0 (?   3 5 =) ? 9

_____

Encode this message.

2. John is my brother.

_____

Write a message in typewriter code on the upper line. Then ask a friend to decode this message and write it in words on the lower line.

3. _____

_____

Activity

▲ If you have access to a computer keyboard, use this same method to create a computer code. Then write a message to a friend in your code.

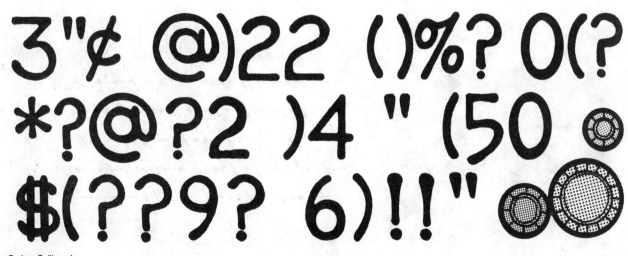

Morse Code

On May 24, 1844, after more than twelve years of experimenting, Samuel F. B. Morse sent a message between Washington, D.C., and Baltimore, Maryland, a distance of about forty miles. The message was sent by wire and traveled at the speed of electricity (186,000 miles per second). It was transmitted instantaneously. The message actually consisted of long and short signals, which Morse made by starting and stopping the flow of electricity through the wire. To the receiver, these signals sounded like rhythmic clicks and rests, but he was quickly able to translate the sounds he heard into letters and to put these letters together to form words. The message sent by the exuberant inventor read, "What hath God wrought!" The instrument Morse had used to control the flow of electricity is called a **magnetic telegraph**. The system of signals he devised for use with this instrument is called **Morse code**.

International Morse Code

A •—	G ——•	N —•	U ••—
B —•••	H ••••	O ———	V •••—
C —•—•	I ••	P •——•	W •——
D —••	J •———	Q ——•—	X —••—
E •	K —•—	R •—•	Y —•——
F ••—•	L •—••	S •••	Z ——••
	M ——	T —	

Comma ——••——   Period •—•—•—

Because it can be difficult to tell where one Morse code letter ends and another begins, people writing in this code often place a single slash (/) between letters and a double slash (//) between words.

Morse code can be used as an auditory code, in which the message is transmitted as sounds, or as a visual code, in which the message is transmitted as flashes of light. In either case, a long signal, or dash, should last the same length of time as three short signals, or dots.

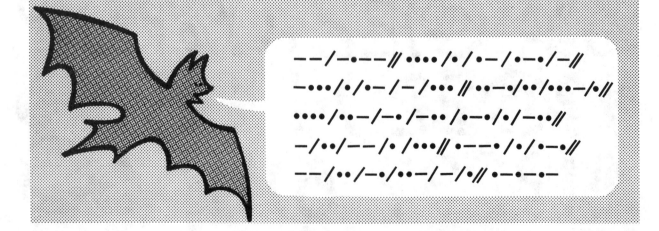

——/—•——// ••••/•/ •—/•—•/—//
—•••/•/•—/—/••• // ••—•/••/•••—/•//
••••/••—/—•/—••/•—•/•/—••//
—/••/—— /• /•••// •——•/•/•—•//
——/••/—•/••—/—/•// •—•—•—

Name _____

Morse Code
(continued)

Decode these messages.

1. ••• / • // ••• / •—•• / • / •——• / —// •—•• / •— / —/ • // •—•—•—

_____

2. ••// •—— / •• / •—•• / •—•• // —— / • / • / —// —•— / ——— / ••— // •— / —//

_____

— / •••• / • // —— / ——— / ••— / •• / • / ••• // •—•—•

_____

Encode these messages.

3. I will help you with your homework.

4. Whistle to the dog.

In the space below, write a message in Morse code. Then hand it to a friend and see if he or she can decode it.

MESSAGE:

Name _____

Building a Telegraph Set

Materials

- ☐ one 12-volt battery
- ☐ 36 meters of thin, insulated copper wire
- ☐ two strips of heavy tin or heavy aluminum 15 cm by 2 cm (The center bottom of a heavy-duty pie pan is perfect.)
- ☐ two strips of heavy tin or heavy aluminum 10 cm by 2 cm
- ☐ kitchen scissors or tin snips
- ☐ two pieces of plywood 17.5 cm by 22 cm and 1.5 cm thick
- ☐ two pieces of wood 4.5 cm square and at least 1.5 cm thick
- ☐ two medium-long nails
- ☐ four long nails
- ☐ six round-headed screws
- ☐ a hammer

Instructions

Do each step *twice* to make two telegraph sets, one for you and one for a friend.

For the Sounder

1. To form the base, use two long nails to attach one piece of wood to a piece of plywood.

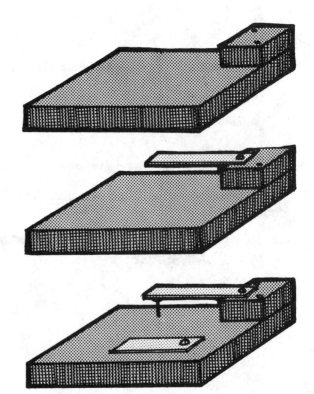

2. Use a nail to punch a hole in one end of one of the longer metal strips. Then attach this strip to the small piece of wood with a screw.

3. Have someone hold up the free end of the metal strip while you hammer one medium-long nail into the base directly under this strip. The space between the strip and the nail head should not be any wider than the thickness of a quarter.

For the Key

1. Use a nail to punch a hole in one end of one of the shorter metal strips. Then fasten this strip to the plywood base with a screw.

Name _____

Building a Telegraph Set
(continued)

2. Bend up the free end of the short metal strip and attach a screw to the base directly under the strip.

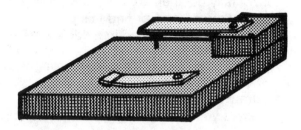

3. Attach the wires *under the strips* to the screws and nails as shown. Wind the wire clockwise around the nail under each sounder about thirty times, forming a tight coil. Be sure that the winding is from bottom to top, ending near the nail head, and that the wire is bare where it is in contact with the nail.

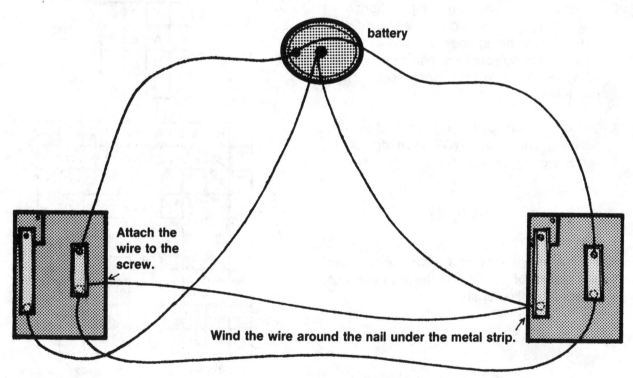

battery

Attach the wire to the screw.

Wind the wire around the nail under the metal strip.

Activities

● 1. Memorize Morse code so that you can send, receive, and decode messages *without* looking at the chart on page 60.

▲⊙2. Use a flashlight to send a message in Morse code to a friend. Ask the friend to write down your message in dots and dashes and then to decode it into letters. Read the message your friend received. Is it the same as the one you sent? Evaluate your sending techniques. How might they be improved to make them more accurate and more reliable?

▲3. Follow the instructions on pages 62 and 63 to build a simple telegraph set. Then use it to send messages in Morse code.

Name _____

Hidden Pathfinder Code

A hidden pathfinder code is one in which the letters of a message are written on a grid horizontally but then are read and copied in a pattern, or along a path. To decode the message, a recipient must know or find this path.

To encode a message in hidden pathfinder code, follow these four steps.

Message: Jack has gone home.

1. Draw a grid large enough to hold all of the letters you will need for your message.

2. Write your message on the grid horizontally, from left to right, one row at a time. If there are open spaces when you have finished writing your message, fill each one with a null letter. In the grid at the right, Z is a null letter.

J	A	C	K
H	A	S	G
O	N	E	H
O	M	E	Z

3. Decide which path you will follow in devising your code. Will it be diagonal, spiral, zigzag, or wavy?

diagonal   **spiral**

zigzag   **wavy**

4. Follow the path you have chosen to write the letters of your message in groups of three, four, five, or six.

Diagonally Encoded Message: JAHO ACKS NOME GHEZ

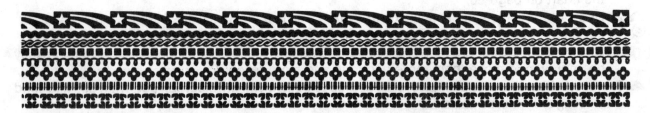

Name _____

Hidden Pathfinder Code
(continued)

Decipher the following messages.

1. **Spiral:** TADT ENST ACEH TKIH

_____

2. **Diagonal:** PAMS YTSB TIEF ERND

_____

Encipher the following messages.

3. **Zigzag:** The circus is here.

_____

4. **Wavy:** Read the comics.

_____

To make it easier for your friends to decipher the messages you write in hidden pathfinder code, devise a series of symbols to stand for the paths you use. For example, you might use a circle or dot (●) to indicate the circular path and a slash mark (/) to indicate the diagonal path. Make a list of these symbols and the paths for which they stand. Give this list to the people who will be decoding your messages. When you encode a message, write the appropriate symbol in front of the message.

Activities

■ 1. Make a chart or poster on which you explain how to create this code.
▲ 2. Design two other pathways through the grid, and give each one a name and symbol.
◉ 3. Compare the diagonal, spiral, zigzag, and wavy patterns. In what ways are they alike? In what ways are they different? Which one is the hardest to follow through the grid? Why?

Name _____

Clue Word Codes

In clue word codes, category words, such as the names of animals, fruits, trees, colors, numbers, or games, are used to call attention to a brief message hidden within a longer text. In the text below, color words are used as clues. The words following the color words form the hidden message.

Longer Text

Dan said that you have been feeling blue. You should take more time to enjoy life. The flowers are in bloom, and the grass is green. Be glad that summer gold's here. Look for a rosy tomorrow.

Hidden Message

You be here tomorrow.

Decode these messages on the lines provided.

1.   We will eat apples tomorrow if the peach is not ripe, but I would prefer berries. A pie might be nice—maybe banana. School starts soon, but we are having a cherry holiday!

_____

2.   At seven come see what I have done to the six over the fireplace. Three to one, my work is done. Mine is the tenth house on the block.

_____

Encode these messages on a separate sheet of paper.

3. We need a soccer ball.
4. It is your turn to bring the cookies.

Activities

■ 1. Make a list of categories and words that you might use in clue word codes. Include at least fifteen words in each category.

▲ 2. Create a worksheet of messages written in clue word codes. See if your classmates can decode them *without* being told the categories of the clue words.

Computer Card Codes

Templates can be used to hide brief messages within longer texts and to find messages that have been hidden in this way. To make a template from a computer or index card or from a piece of tagboard, carefully cut out rectangular holes that are the size of words and that will allow insertion of your message. To hide a message, lay the template on a piece of paper, write or type the message within the holes, remove the template, and add surrounding words to mislead an unauthorized reader.

Brief Message   Longer Text

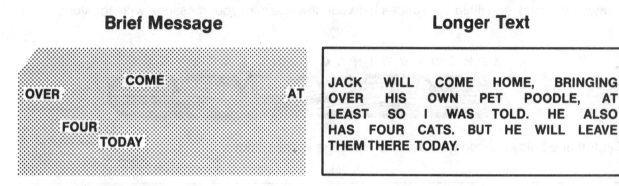

COME
OVER   AT
FOUR
TODAY

JACK WILL COME HOME, BRINGING OVER HIS OWN PET POODLE, AT LEAST SO I WAS TOLD. HE ALSO HAS FOUR CATS. BUT HE WILL LEAVE THEM THERE TODAY.

Using the template pictured above, find the brief message hidden in this longer text, and write it on the line below.

THEY PLAY HIDE AND SEEK, AND IT LOOKS LIKE FUN, BUT NOT IN THE CACTUS GARDEN. THEY RAN INTO THE BACKYARD, AND SEVERAL KIDS HID IN THE BUSHES.

Activities

▲ 1. Design several templates for use in finding hidden messages.
▲ 2. Use these templates to hide brief messages within longer texts that make sense.
▲ 3. Use punched computer cards to hide separate letters of a word or message.

Name _____

Popsicle Stick Code

Popsicle sticks can be used to encode and decode messages. You need a minimum of two matched sticks, one for the person sending the coded message and one for the person receiving it. To prepare the sticks, cut off one end of each stick so that it is straight. Then, with the straight end on the left, notch or mark the upper edge of the stick in several places. To encode a message, lay the Popsicle stick on a piece of paper and draw a guideline along the straight end of the stick. Holding the stick firmly at this guideline, write the letters of the message above the notches or marks. Then remove the stick and fill in the spaces between the letters of your message with additional letters.

S H O U L D W I N A G R A N D R A C E Y E T

On the line below, decode the sample message written above.

_____

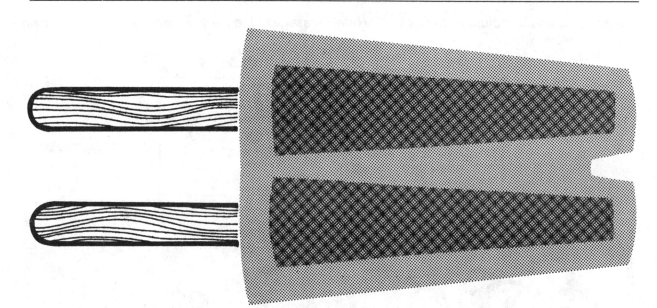

Activities

▲ 1. Notch several pairs of Popsicle sticks for use in decoding and encoding messages. Mark both members of each pair with the same letter, number, or symbol so that they can be easily matched for encoding and decoding purposes. Store these sticks in a coffee can or other similar tall, widemouthed container.

▲ 2. One pair of Popsicle sticks will enable you to encode and decode a word or two, or to encode and decode longer messages written on several lines if the message letter placement remains the same. Create a series of sticks for use with longer messages in which the message letter placement is varied from line to line. Letter or number these sticks so that both the person sending the message and the person receiving it will know the order in which the sticks should be used.

■ 3. Create a code based on some other common and inexpensive household object.

Name _____

Paper Clip Code

Paper clips can be used to encode and decode messages. Lay a No. 1 paper clip sideways on your paper with the double loop on the right. Write the first letter of your message between the loops at the double-looped (right-hand) end of the clip. Then move the clip to the right until the left-hand end overlaps the letter you just wrote. Again, write a letter between the loops at the right-hand end. Continue in this manner until you have written out your entire message. Then remove the paper clip and fill the spaces between the letters of the message with additional letters.

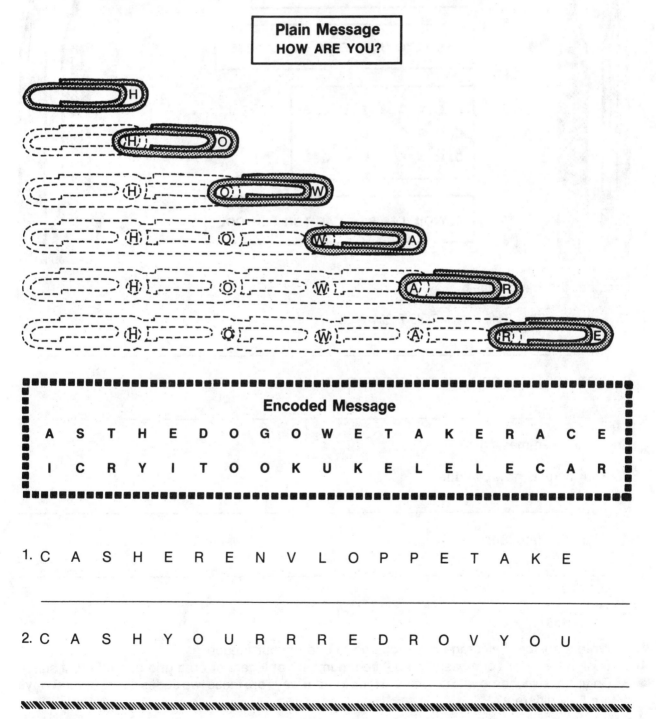

```
Plain Message
HOW ARE YOU?
```

Encoded Message

A	S	T	H	E	D	O	G	O	W	E	T	A	K	E	R	A	C	E
I	C	R	Y	I	T	O	O	K	U	K	E	L	E	L	E	C	A	R

1. C A S H E R E N V L O P P E T A K E

_____

2. C A S H Y O U R R R E D R O V Y O U

_____

Switcheroo

Encoding in switcheroo is a four-step process. First, write out your message. Second, divide this message into an even number of groups of four letters. Add null letters in any group that has fewer than four letters. Third, print the letters on the grid as shown. Fourth, write the letters horizontally in groups of three.

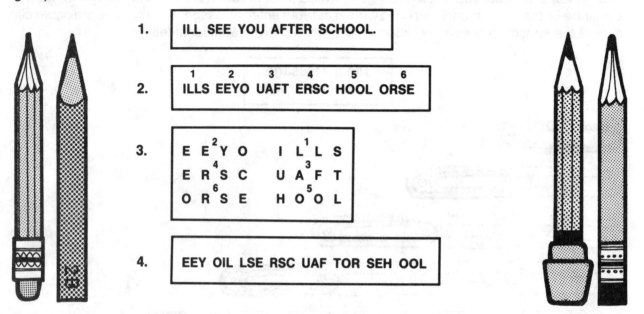

1. ILL SEE YOU AFTER SCHOOL.

2. | 1 | 2 | 3 | 4 | 5 | 6 |
ILLS EEYO UAFT ERSC HOOL ORSE

3.
E E²Y O   I L¹L S
E R⁴S C   U A³F T
O R⁶S E   H O⁵O L

4. EEY OIL LSE RSC UAF TOR SEH OOL

Decipher these messages.

1. EYI STH EKR THE UND EOL PQM ATZ

_____

2. GOT ABI LLE NSP NEW TIK EZE EDB

_____

Encipher these messages.

3. Your book is now overdue.

_____

4. I'll treat you to lunch.

_____

Activities

▲ 1. Write a postcard message in switcheroo to one of your friends.
▲ 2. Design a similar code based on different numbers of letters or on a grid of a different size.
■ 3. Compare switcheroo with columns of four. In what ways are these two codes alike? In what ways are they different?

Name _____

The Greek Code

To encode messages in the Greek code, you need a strip of paper and a stick, dowel, or pencil. Wrap the strip of paper around the pencil, making certain that each new wrap touches the previous one but does *not* overlap. When the entire strip of paper has been wrapped, print your message from one end of the pencil to the other across the wrapped strip. Unwind the strip before delivering your message.

To decode your message, the person receiving it must have an identical stick, dowel, or pencil and must wrap the strip in the same way. He or she will then find that the message is clearly readable.

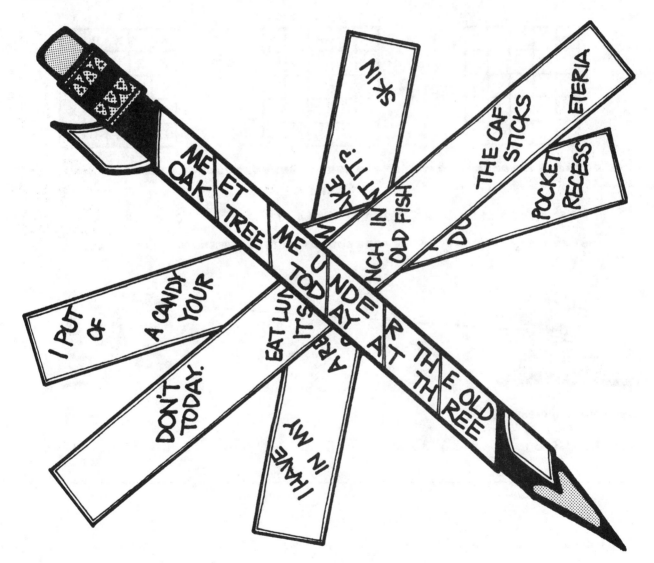

Activities

1. Make a labeled chart or poster for your classroom on which you explain what Greek code is and how it is used.
2. Use this code to exchange messages with some of your classmates.
3. List some other readily available objects that might be used for encoding and decoding messages in Greek code.

Name _____

Coordinate Code

The basic idea for this code goes all the way back to the ancient Greeks, who used a similar grid for some of their codes. To encipher a message, first draw a five-square-by-five-square grid. Second, number the columns across the top and the rows down the left-hand side. Third, write the letters of the alphabet in the squares of the grid as shown. Fourth, encipher the letters of your message by writing their grid coordinates. Write the horizontal coordinate first, followed by the vertical coordinate. For example, *R* would be 4 *over* from the left and 3 *down* from the top, or 4,3.

Message: Take the dog home.

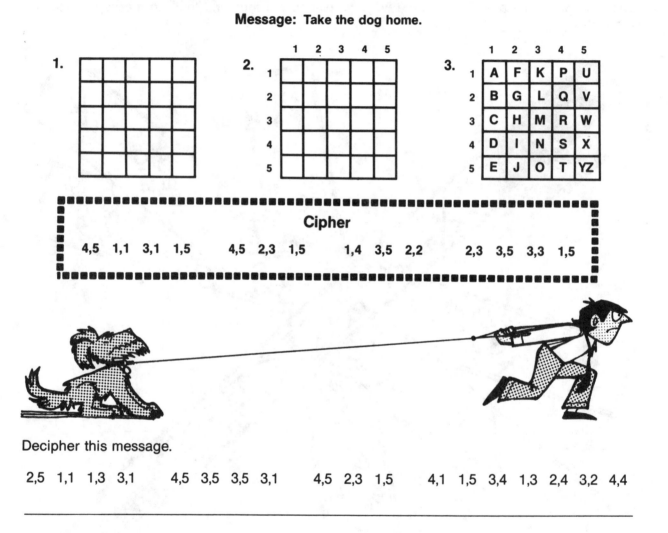

	1	2	3	4	5
1	A	F	K	P	U
2	B	G	L	Q	V
3	C	H	M	R	W
4	D	I	N	S	X
5	E	J	O	T	YZ

Cipher

4,5 1,1 3,1 1,5   4,5 2,3 1,5   1,4 3,5 2,2   2,3 3,5 3,3 1,5

Decipher this message.

2,5 1,1 1,3 3,1   4,5 3,5 3,5 3,1   4,5 2,3 1,5   4,1 1,5 3,4 1,3 2,4 3,2 4,4

_____

Activities

▲1. Use coordinates to write a message.

■ 2. Compare this code with columns of four (on page 46). In what ways are these two codes alike? In what ways are they different?

■ 3. A five-by-five grid is actually one square short for the twenty-six letter English alphabet. This
★   problem is solved by allowing the letters *Y* and *Z* to share a square. Would the Greek alphabet
◉   have fit better in a grid of this size? Explain your answer.

Name _____

Posttest

Decipher each of the following encoded messages on the first line. Then write the name of the code in which the message is written on the second line.

1. ••—/•••/•//— /••••/••/••• //—•—•/———/—••/• // •——/••/—/•••• //
•—// —/•/•—••/•/——• /•—•/•—•/•——•/•••• //••• /• / — //

   _____

   _____

2. ONE LITTLE BLUE FOURTEEN HOUSE SAW RED PEOPLE WHO WERE PURPLE CAME IN
   THE ROOM

   _____

   _____

3. ⊡⌐⊓ᴗᴗᴗ< ⊡ᴖ⌐⊡ᴖ⊡ ⌐ᴖ ᴖᴦ•⊡

   _____

   _____

4. NBSZ IBE B MJUUMF MBNC

   _____

   _____

5.
3 dish soap	1 bag apples
2 jars thyme	2 bunches spinach
1 doz. eggs	2 boxes rice mix
2 lbs. margarine	3 small pizzas
3 cans cat food	1 lb. zucchini
3 gal. ice cream	2 lbs. lamb

   _____

   _____

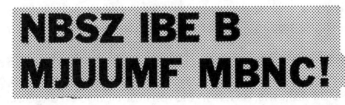

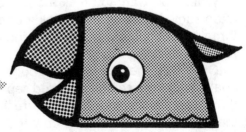

Name _____

Delivering Messages

Sometimes the most challenging part of sending a coded message is finding a novel way to deliver it. At home, if you have a cat or dog that will go to the person to whom you are sending the message, then a good place to hide your message is under the pet's collar. If you are fortunate enough to have homing pigeons, you have the perfect mailmen for your messages. And you can always enclose a hidden message in a letter.

In the classroom, messages can be tucked inside the cover of a book, in a coat or jacket pocket, under the brim of a cap or hat, or in a lunch box or sack. Outside, messages can be left in a hollow tree trunk, hidden under a rock, folded inside bicycle handlebars, or lodged between the bricks in a wall. The possibilities are endless. Just be certain that the person to whom you are sending the message knows when and where to look.

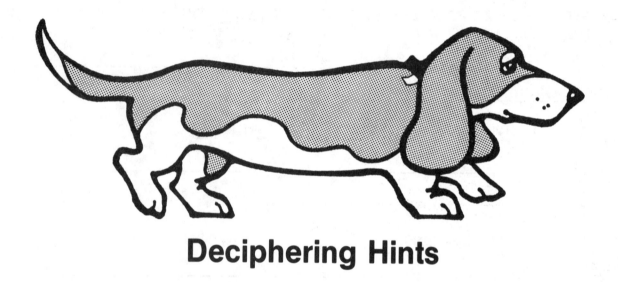

Deciphering Hints

Before there were computers to help decipher messages, cryptographers spent weeks, months, and even years trying to crack a single code. Among the clues they used were the frequency of individual letters and the patterns of letter combinations. For example, the letter *E* is the most frequently used letter in the English language. It appears in more than half of all words and 126 times in every 1,000 letters. The next most common letters are *T, O, A,* and *N.* After *T,* the letters *R, D,* and *S* are the most frequently used consonants. *N* is the consonant that most often follows a vowel. *T* is the consonant most commonly used to begin a word, and *E* is the letter most often found at the end of a word. The consonants *D* and *N* are also frequently used to end words.

The only one-letter words in the English language are *A* and *I.* The most frequently used two-letter words are prepositions—*of, to,* and *in. The* and *and* are the most frequently used three-letter words, and *that* is the most common four-letter word.

When you want to break a code, begin by looking for one- and two-letter words. Notice how often some letters appear. Look for double vowels or consonants and for common two-letter and three-letter endings. Incidentally, the three-letter endings most frequently used in English are *ing, ion,* and *ant.*

Obviously, the way to make a code more difficult to break is to design it so that it defies this sort of analysis. Letters can be encoded separately, as they are in the key word match code on page 50, or their order can be varied to obscure these clue patterns, as it is in the rail fence code on page 52, in the hidden pathfinder code on pages 64-65, and in switcheroo on page 70.

Invisible Inks

Invisible inks are liquids that can be used for writing, that fade or disappear as they dry, and that can be made to reappear by exposure to heat or to a particular chemical solution. Simple invisible inks include lemon juice and vinegar. Both of these liquids will disappear as they dry and then reappear when exposed to heat. Either a 150-watt light bulb or a laundry iron can be a good source of heat, but be careful not to burn yourself or to scorch your paper. Also, some of these ink solutions have a bleaching effect and/or may adversely affect paper dyes. For this reason, they will be much more effective if used on plain white paper.

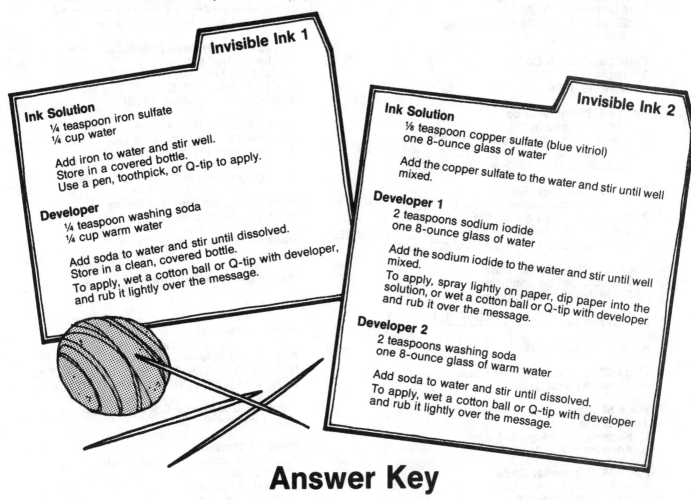

Invisible Ink 1

Ink Solution
¼ teaspoon iron sulfate
¼ cup water

Add iron to water and stir well.
Store in a covered bottle.
Use a pen, toothpick, or Q-tip to apply.

Developer
¼ teaspoon washing soda
¼ cup warm water

Add soda to water and stir until dissolved.
Store in a clean, covered bottle.
To apply, wet a cotton ball or Q-tip with developer, and rub it lightly over the message.

Invisible Ink 2

Ink Solution
⅛ teaspoon copper sulfate (blue vitriol)
one 8-ounce glass of water

Add the copper sulfate to the water and stir until well mixed.

Developer 1
2 teaspoons sodium iodide
one 8-ounce glass of water

Add the sodium iodide to the water and stir until well mixed.
To apply, spray lightly on paper, dip paper into the solution, or wet a cotton ball or Q-tip with developer and rub it over the message.

Developer 2
2 teaspoons washing soda
one 8-ounce glass of warm water

Add soda to water and stir until dissolved.
To apply, wet a cotton ball or Q-tip with developer and rub it lightly over the message.

Answer Key

Page 43, Pretest
1. D 2. J 3. G 4. E 5. H 6. I 7. F 8. B 9. A
10. C
Underlined numbers: 11, 12, 13
19. Please come home.
20. Jump on the bandwagon.

Page 46, Columns of Four
1. What grade are you in? (*Null letters:* Y,S,T)
2. Marianne has the book. (*Null letters:* S,P)
3. GBA OER TDL OEY
4. WHOAU ATDTR TVAFS CTYOP
   (*Null letters:* S, P)

Pages 47-48, Shopping List Codes
1. Joe has it.
   (*Hint:* The number at the front of each line indicates the letter that should be read for that line.)
2. Her name is Lyn.
   (*Hint:* The first number in the list indicates the significant letter position for all of the entries that follow.)

Page 49, Caesar's Code
1. This is a variation of Caesar's code.
2. This code has a shift of fifteen.

Pages 50-51, Key Word Match Code
1. Happy New Year!
2. The dog is asleep.
3. ZGY ACEZGY AOOW C XIWWL
4. LJL DOAWTZ PZPO CDOM

Page 52, Rail Fence Code
1. We have a substitute today.
   (*Null letters:* D, Z)
2. SEOA ANET SUGT NOHR ETAB
   (*Null letters:* A, B)

Page 53, Name It Code
1. Help!
2. Answers will vary.

Page 54, Phone-a-Code
1. Use the phone buttons.
2. I like horses and dogs.
3. 3·73·3 4·2·7· 9·6·87 ·7362·4·5·
4. ·33735 4·7· 7·4·2·5 ·86·3·29·

Page 55, Tick-Tack-Toe Code
1. Columbus discovered America.
2. Washington was our first president.
3. VDCCOQEЏ UЏ⅄ꓶꓶꓶ ⅄ꓶᗡ ⟨ЏⱯᒧEᒧᒧᒧ ьᖆᗞᒪꓵᒧEᗞ
4. ᒪᒧ⟨ᒪᒪЏᗞᒪᒧᒧ ᒧᒪE ⋀ᒧᒪ⟨ ⋀ᒧEᒧᒪЏЄ

Page 56, Triple Threat Code
1. The dots can be confusing.
2. Triple threat is like pigpen.
3. ꓤꟽꟽᒧ ᖷᒧꓶ ꓭ ᗷꟽᖷ ꓵꓶᗶᒪ ᗷᒪᒪᖷᗷ
4. ꓶᒪᒪ ꓵᖷᗷᖷᗷᒪꓶᗷ ᖷᒪ ꓵᗷᖷᒪᗷ

Page 57, Crossword Clues Code
Put head on desk at two.

Page 58, Symbolic Code
1. He broke his leg.
2. ☾ ✳☾☺✦ ♀♡♣♡✖☾✦☆♬
3. Answers will vary.

Page 59, Typewriter Code
1. Let's go to the movies.
2. *5(4)9 3§ #850(?8
3. Answers will vary.

Pages 60-61, Morse Code
1. He slept late.
2. I will meet you at the movies.
3. ··▪/━━/·· /·━━/ ·━━ ▪▪ ··▪/·/·━━/·━━ ▪▪
   ━·━━/━━━/ ·━· ▪▪ ━━/··/·━━/
   ━·━━/━━━/ ·━· /━· ▪▪ ···· /━━━/━━/··/
   ·━━/━━━/ ·━·/··/━· ▪▪ ·━··━
4. ·━━/····/·· /··· /━/·━·/· ▪▪ ━/━━━▪▪
   ━/····/· ▪▪ ··/━━━ /━━·▪▪ ·━·━·━

Pages 64-65, Hidden Pathfinder Code
1. The cat had kittens.
2. Pat's my best friend.
3. CEHT IRCU HSIS EREZ
4. RTOS AMHE AEIX BCCD

Page 66, Clue Word Codes
1. Tomorrow is a school holiday!
2. Come over to my house.
3. Answers will vary.
4. Answers will vary.

Page 67, Computer Card Codes
Hide it in the bushes.

Page 68, Popsicle Stick Code
Hungry

Page 69, Paper Clip Code
1. Help!
2. Hurry!

Page 70, Switcheroo
1. The key is under the mat.
2. Bill got a new ten-speed bike.
3. BOO KYO URW OVE ISN OOO OOR DUE
4. REA TIL LTO LUN YOU TOO OOC HOO

Page 72, Coordinate Code
Jack took the pencils.

Page 73, Posttest
1. Use this code with a telegraph set.
   Morse code
2. Fourteen people came.
   clue word code
3. School starts at nine.
   tick-tack-toe code
4. Mary had a little lamb.
   shift code
5. She ate a pizza.
   shopping list code

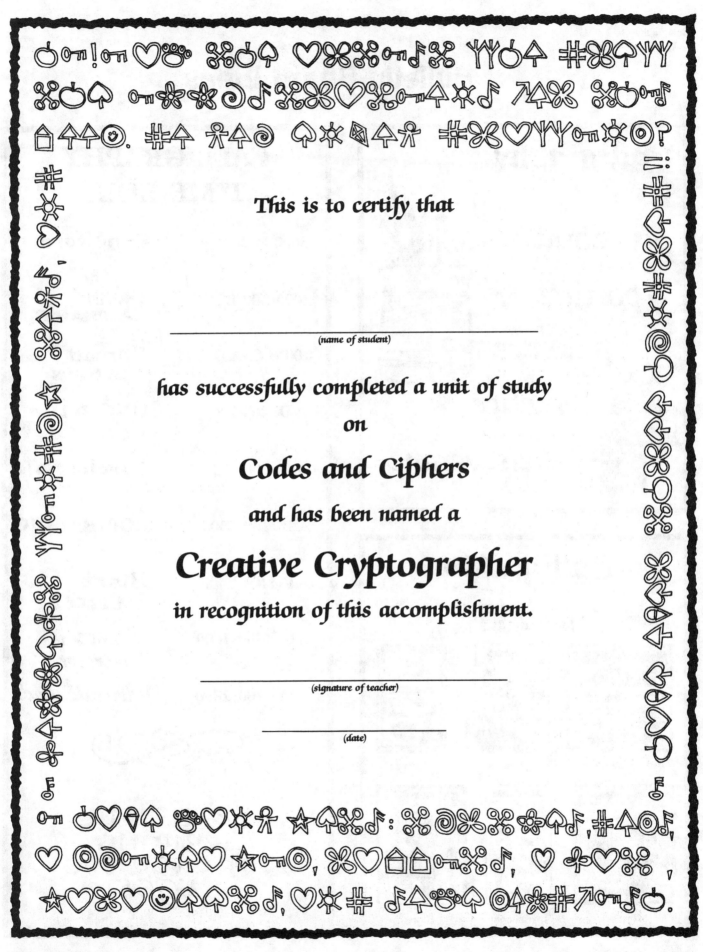

This is to certify that

_____
(name of student)

has successfully completed a unit of study

on

Codes and Ciphers

and has been named a

Creative Cryptographer

in recognition of this accomplishment.

_____
(signature of teacher)

_____
(date)

Bulletin Board Ideas

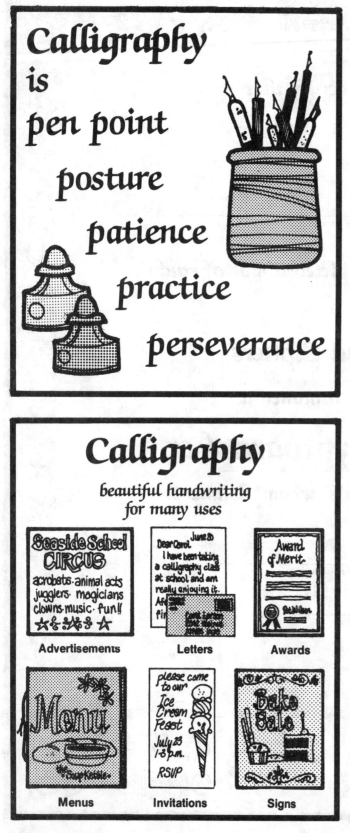

Calligraphy
is
pen point
posture
patience
practice
perseverance

Calligraphy
beautiful handwriting
for many uses

Advertisements

Letters

Awards

Menus

Invitations

Signs

CALLIGRAPHY TIME LINE

3000 B.C.	Cuneiform
1000-500 B.C.	Greek Alphabet
100 B.C.-A.D. 500	Roman Letters
A.D. 200-700	Uncial
A.D. 700-900	Carolingian
A.D. 1100-1300	Lombardic
A.D. 1100-1400	Black Letter
A.D. 1400-1600	Chancery Cursive
A.D. 1700-1850	Roundhand

BEAUTIFUL WRITING THROUGH THE AGES

Learning Center Ideas

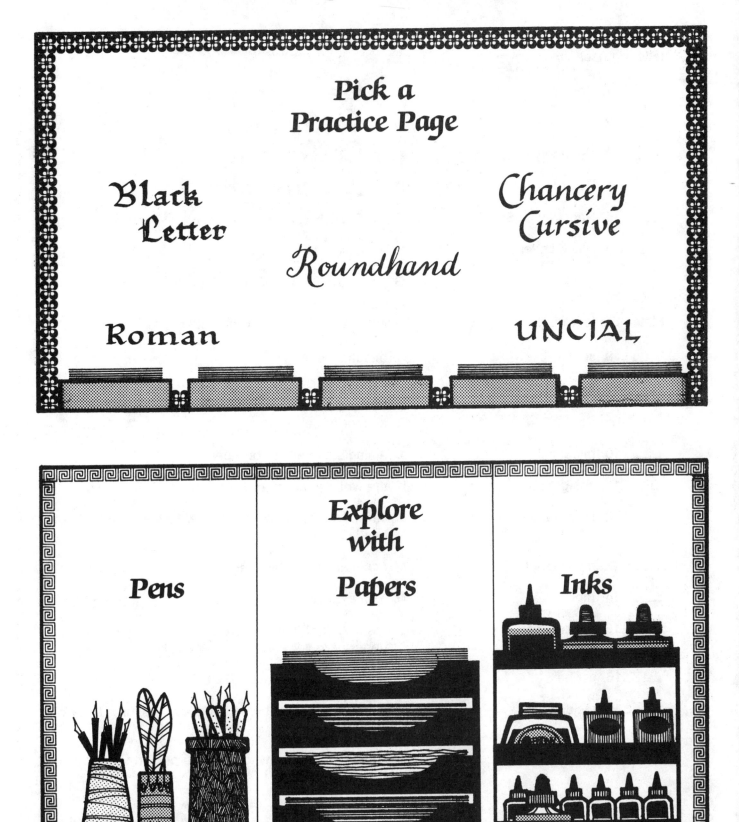

Pick a
Practice Page

Black
Letter

Chancery
Cursive

Roundhand

Roman

UNCIAL

Explore
with

Pens

Papers

Inks

Name _____

Pretest

Identify the different styles in which the word **calligraphy** has been written by writing the correct letter on each line.

____ 1. Roman

____ 2. Roundhand

____ 3. Chancery Cursive

____ 4. Batarde

____ 5. Roman with Serif

____ 6. Black Letter

____ 7. Uncial

A. Calligraphy

B. Calligraphy

C. Calligraphy

D. Calligraphy

E. Calligraphy

F. Calligraphy

G. CALLIGRAPHY

Match the following words with their definitions by writing the correct letter on each line.

____ 8. serif

____ 9. ascender

____ 10. minuscule

____ 11. calligraphy

____ 12. illumination

____ 13. manuscript

____ 14. nib

____ 15. descender

____ 16. scribe

____ 17. majuscule

____ 18. scriptorium

____ 19. stroke

____ 20. text

H. beautiful writing

I. hand decoration of a manuscript page with elaborate designs and miniature pictures drawn in bright colors and/or in gold

J. a single movement of a pen

K. the writing end of a pen

L. part of a letter that extends *below* the main body of that letter

M. material written by hand

N. a small writing room

O. a short, light line that projects at an angle from the upper or lower end of a letter stroke

P. an uppercase, or capital, letter

Q. part of a letter that extends *above* the main body of that letter

R. literally, a person who writes; a person who copied books by hand

S. the words that are written

T. a lowercase letter

Name _____

Early Alphabets

Ancient people had no way to write their words or to record their thoughts. What they could not remember was useless. What they could not retell was soon lost. At first, they used symbols or pictures to represent ideas, objects, and events. As early as 3000 B.C., the Egyptians used **hieroglyphics**, or picture writing, to record their thoughts. Then, a little before 1000 B.C., the Phoenicians, who lived northeast of Egypt, developed an alphabet of consonants.

An **alphabet** is a system of letters used to represent the different sounds in a language. The word **alphabet** is made up of two Greek words, **alpha** and **beta**, the first two letters of the Greek alphabet. The Greeks adopted the Phoenician alphabet and added vowels to it, thus making twenty-four letters. Shortly thereafter, the Romans borrowed the Greek alphabet and changed it into the Roman capital letters we know today. All of the letters we use are based on the Roman alphabet.

The Greek Alphabet

A α	alpha	H η	eta	N ν	nu	T τ	tau
B β	beta	Θ θ	theta	Ξ ξ	xi	Υ υ	upsilon
Γ γ	gamma	I ι	iota	O o	omicron	Φ φ	phi
Δ δ	delta	K κ	kappa	Π π	pi	X χ	chi
E ε	epsilon	Λ λ	lambda	P ρ	rho	Ψ ψ	psi
Z ζ	zeta	M μ	mu	Σ σς	sigma	Ω ω	omega

Activities

■ 1. Read about hieroglyphics. Then describe what they are and how they were used.

■ 2. The Rosetta stone, found in 1799, helped unravel the mystery of Egyptian hieroglyphics. Because a single message had been written on it in hieroglyphics, demotic characters, and Greek, scholars were able to decipher a system of writing that had previously been incomprehensible. Do some research to learn more about the Rosetta stone. Then explain how and why it was so valuable to scholars.

▲ 3. Make an alphabet time line on which you indicate important dates and events in the development of written language.

★ 4. Look at the letters of the Greek alphabet. Then make a chart on which you show which Greek letters are like ours and which ones are different.

★ 5. Make a chart on which you show how letters that are common to several alphabets have evolved over the years.

Name _____

Calligraphy

The word **calligraphy** comes from two Greek words: **kalos**, meaning "beautiful," and **graphos**, meaning "written" or "writing." Thus, calligraphy means "beautiful writing."

For many centuries, before the invention of the typewriter or the printing press, all manuscripts were copied by hand. It was important for them to be both beautiful and readable. Writers took great care in forming the letters and words. Some of them even decorated, or **illuminated**, their manuscripts with elaborate designs and miniature pictures painted in gold, silver, and brilliant colors. Monks in monasteries copied chapters and books from the Bible. Special **scribes**, or **calligraphers**, were hired by courts and governments to copy books and to hand-letter important documents and proclamations.

Then, in the fifteenth century, a German printer named Johann Gutenberg invented a method of printing from movable type. Suddenly, monks and scribes were no longer needed to copy books. The printing press could do their job faster and more accurately. The companion arts of calligraphy and manuscript illumination were all but lost.

The art of fine handwriting gradually disappeared. People came to rely heavily on the typewriter and, more recently, on the word processor. They ceased to practice penmanship and, in some instances, developed an almost illegible script.

Today, there is a revival of interest in calligraphy and in other "beautiful writing." Modern typefaces have been designed to look like old-fashioned calligraphic scripts. Calligraphers, who are also called **penmen**, are being hired to hand-letter diplomas, degrees, other documents, and limited-edition books. Perhaps, after this unit, you will become part of the return to fine handwriting known as the calligraphy revival.

Activities

● 1. The most famous book printed by Gutenberg on his press was the Bible. Only a few of the Bibles he printed are still in existence. Most of them are in museum manuscript and book collections. If possible, visit such a collection to view a Gutenberg Bible and, perhaps, some hand-copied and/or illuminated manuscripts.

★ 2. You are familiar with the Greek words **graphos** and **kalos**. On a separate sheet of paper, list fifteen English words that have been made from either one of these Greek words, look up the words you have listed in a dictionary, and write their meanings beside them. For example, what is a **kaleidoscope**?

★ 3. The English word **legible** comes from the Latin word **lego**, **legere**, meaning "to read." The English word **script** comes from the Latin word **scribo**, **scribere**, meaning "to draw or write." On a separate sheet of paper, list fifteen words that contain one of these Latin words, look up the words you have listed in a dictionary, and write their meanings beside them. For example, what is **script**? What does a **scribe** do? What do you do when you **scribble**? When is a **prescription** written?

Name _____

Tools

If you are going to be a calligrapher, your main tool will be a broad-edged pen. Calligraphic pens are available in stationery and art supply stores. They come in dip, cartridge, fountain, and felt-tipped models. Only time and experience will tell you which kind works best for you. An inexpensive way to begin is by purchasing a penholder and at least two Speedball points designated with the letter *C*. Choose either *C-1, C-2, C-3,* or *C-4*. Companies like Osmiroid, Platignum, and Sheaffer make good cartridge and fountain pens. Felt-tipped calligraphic pens are available from Sanford, and Pentel makes refillable cartridge color brushes that may be used for brush writing, calligraphy, or illumination.

In addition to pens, you will also need a drawing board (a bread board will do), a desk or steady table on which to prop or rest the board, a straight but comfortable stool or chair, a good lamp, a T-square, a ruler, a triangle, a blotter, and some old rags. For best results, keep the board on a slant, and cover it with several sheets of paper, a desk blotter, or a piece of cardboard to make the surface softer. Keep your tools clean. You cannot do clean, finished work either with a dirty pen or in a messy area.

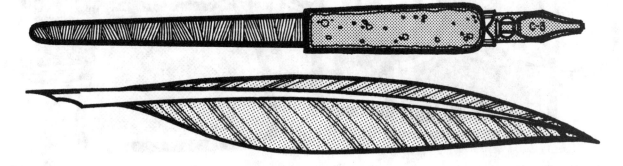

Activities

● 1. Visit a library or a museum in which hand-copied books and handwritten documents are displayed. Make a note of the dates given for these books and documents, and notice how the formation of individual letters and the overall style of handwriting have changed through the years. How might available writing implements have influenced writing style?

▲ 2. Before ballpoint, cartridge, felt-tipped, and fountain pens were available, people wrote with **quills,** or feather pens. To make a quill pen, they trimmed the pointed end of a horny, hollow feather shaft on a slant. To write, they dipped this end, called the **nib**, into a bottle or well of ink. The pen had to be dipped frequently, and care had to be taken not to drop splotches, or blots, of ink on the paper. Cut off the pointed end of a feather shaft to make a quill pen. Then write with it.

◉ 3. Write with several different kinds of pens. Compare the pens, and evaluate the results you obtain with each. Choose the one you like best, and defend your choice in writing.

Name _____

Materials

For good results, use only good materials. Cheap paper bleeds, and cheap ink runs. A 20-pound white bond paper will work nicely for practice; but for your finished work, you will want to buy parchment or some other fine quality art or stationery paper.

The ink you select should be of medium thickness. If it is too thin and watery, it will run. If it is too thick, it may flow unevenly and cause your writing to look clumsy. If you are using black, it should be very black. If you are using a color, it should be consistent. You do not want an ink that is unpredictable, that goes on differently or dries differently each time.

India ink is of good quality, but it is waterproof. If you use it, you will need to be very careful to put it only where you want it because it will not wash out. Also, you may find that waterproof inks are thicker and tend to clog your pens. Some water-soluble fountain pen inks are as color-true as waterproof inks, but are thinner and flow more evenly. They are less inclined to clog and will wash out of your pen reservoir or off your pen point in cold water.

If you are using Speedball points or other points with ink reservoirs, purchase your ink in bottles that have droppers. These droppers will enable you to fill the reservoirs quickly and neatly.

In addition to ink and paper, you may wish to keep on hand a roll of drafting or masking tape to use in anchoring the paper on which you are working.

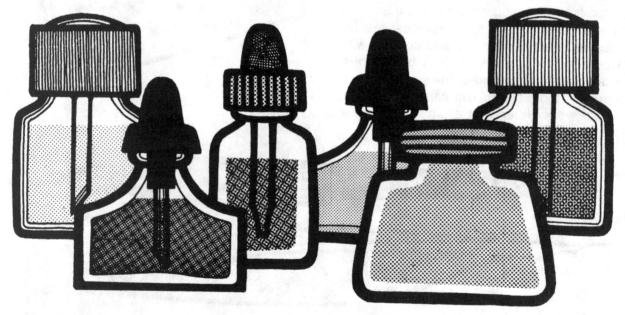

Activities

● 1. Do some research to discover what people wrote on before they had paper. When, where, and by whom was paper first made?

● 2. Do some research to discover what liquid substances people have used to write with. When, where, and by whom was ink first used?

■ 3. Read about how paper is made today. Then create a diagram or chart on which you draw pictures of the steps involved in making paper and label them.

■ 4. Find out how colored inks are made today. Write a description of this process.

▲ 5. Make colored ink from some natural substance like blueberries. Use this ink to write the recipe for the ink you made.

■ 6. Compare the inks used in pens with those used on printing presses. In what ways are they alike? In what ways are they different? Why?

Writing Position

In calligraphy, correct body and paper position are extremely important and will have a marked influence on your results. Because calligraphy must be done relatively slowly, you will want to be in a position that is comfortable, one in which you can work for a long period of time. Prop your drawing board up so that it is on a slant. Adjust your chair or stool so that you can sit straight and face your board directly. If you are right-handed, place a light on your left and the ink bottle on your right. If you are left-handed, reverse this placement. Put your paper on the board, use your T-square to be certain that it is straight, and then tape all four corners in place with drafting or masking tape. As you work, hold your pen at a high angle and write slowly.

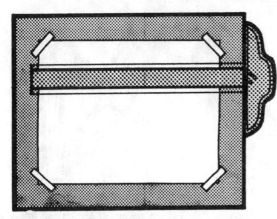

Make certain your paper is straight, then tape it to your board.

Hold your pen at a high angle (about 30 to 35 degrees) as you work.

Sit straight and face your slanted board directly.

Activities

1. Experiment with your writing position. Adjust the height at which you sit mechanically or by adding books or pillows to your stool or chair. Take measurements, compare results, and discover what height is best for *you*. You should sit so that you are both alert and comfortable.

2. Experiment with the angle of your drawing board. Set the board, measure the angle, then write and label a handwriting sample. Repeat this procedure several times, changing the board angle each time. Try it once more with the board perfectly flat. Compare your results. How did the angle of the board affect *your* writing?

Name _____

Getting Started

Once you have set up your work area, it is time to begin. If you are using a dip pen, it will have a **reservoir** between the tip and the top cover, or **tongue**. Using an ink dropper, fill this reservoir about half full of ink. To avoid putting ink blots on your finished work, write first on a practice sheet of paper to get the ink flowing. When writing, place the pen firmly on the paper, making sure that the entire writing edge of the pen is in contact with the paper. If you roll the pen to the right, the left side of your calligraphy will be ragged and/or blurred. If you roll the pen to the left, the right side of your calligraphy will not be sharp and clean. To produce clean edges, you must rest your pen fully and firmly on the paper. As you write, keep your pen at a 30- to 35-degree angle. Make slow, careful strokes, holding your breath during each stroke to keep your hand from shaking.

For dip pen points with ink reservoirs, purchase ink in bottles that have droppers.

Use a dropper to fill the ink reservoir located between the tip and the top cover, or tongue.

Fill the reservoir about half full of a good quality ink.

Activities

● 1. Practice filling and cleaning your pen.
● 2. Repeat each one of these strokes until it feels natural.

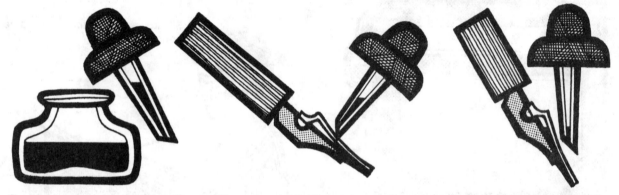

● 3. Try some of these practice patterns.

Name _____

Beginning Alphabets

Thus far in school, you have learned to write in two alphabets—the **manuscript**, or printed, alphabet and the **cursive**, or written, alphabet. Write each one of these alphabets on the lines below.

Manuscript Alphabet

Aa

Cursive Alphabet

Aa

In this calligraphy unit, you will learn two more alphabets—**Roman** and **Chancery Cursive**—that are very much like the two alphabets you already know.

Activities

1. Make a large chart for your classroom showing the manuscript and cursive alphabets.
2. Compare the ways cursive is taught in two or more different handwriting or penmanship textbooks. Are the styles the same, slightly different, or very different? In what years were these books published? Does handwriting style vary with time?
3. Compare the manuscript and cursive alphabets. In what ways are they similar? In what ways are they different?
4. If possible, obtain a penmanship textbook that is at least fifty years old. Compare the letter examples in this book with similar examples from a more recent penmanship textbook. In what ways are they alike? In what ways are they different? Is the taught (and accepted) handwriting style being simplified or is it becoming more ornate? Which style is more pleasing to the eye? Which style is easier to write? Which style is easier to read?

Name _____

Roman Majuscules

The first alphabet you will learn is called **Roman**. In this alphabet, there are two types of letters, capital letters, called **majuscules**, and lowercase letters, called **minuscules**. To create letters in the Roman style, you must be very careful about two things—vertical lines and horizontal spacing. In this style, most of the straight letter lines should be perpendicular to the line on which you are writing, and very little space should be left between letters. Only the width of a lowercase *o* separates individual words.

Using your T-square and your pen tip, draw four guidelines for your work. Use the width of your pen tip to determine the space between these lines. The lines should be drawn so that there are three pen widths between the bottom line and the second line, five pen widths between the second line and the third line, and four pen widths between the third line and the top line.

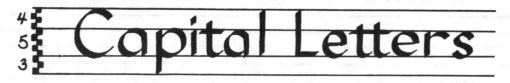

The middle space is where you write the word, the top space is for capital letters and for the **ascenders** of tall letters like *t* and *l*, and the lower space is for the **descenders** of letters like *p*.

Note how the Roman majuscules below are formed. Then slowly practice writing each one of them. Make certain that your letters stand up tall and straight.

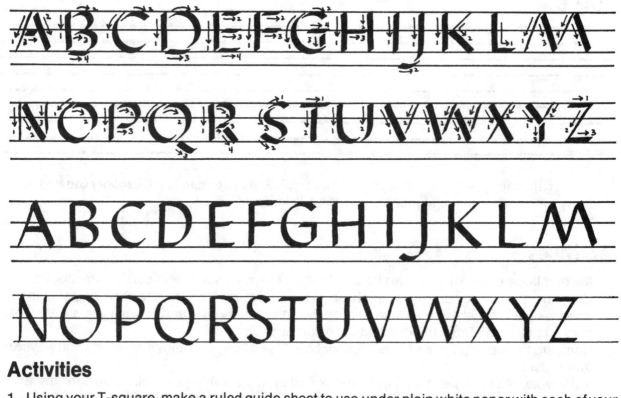

Activities

▲ 1. Using your T-square, make a ruled guide sheet to use under plain white paper with each of your pens or pen tips. Label each sheet with the appropriate pen name, letter, and number so that you will know when to use it.

▲ 2. Look up a proverb or epigram and copy it on paper using Roman majuscules.

Name _____

Roman Minuscules

Most Roman minuscules are formed in the middle writing space. The letter *t* is different from all of the others. It extends above the middle space, but only slightly. Note how the Roman minuscules below are formed. Then, slowly practice writing each one of them.

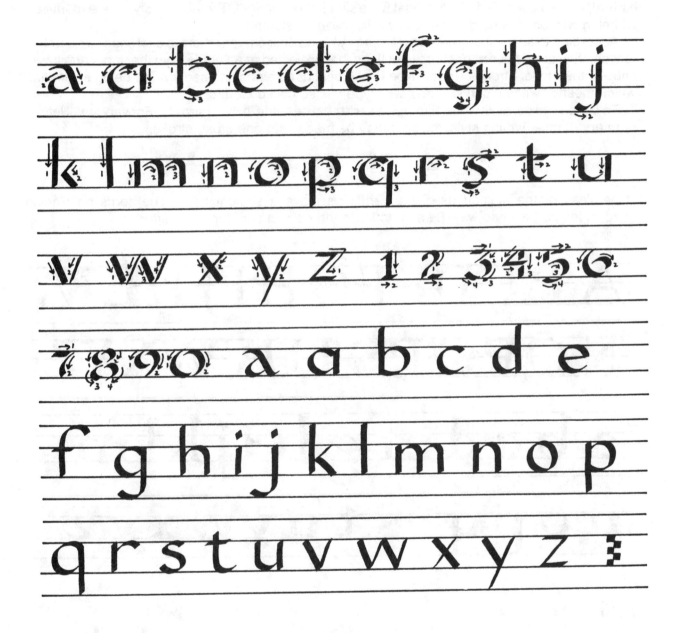

Activities

▲ 1. Make a large chart that teaches a spelling concept. Use the Roman alphabet. Post this chart in your bedroom at home or in your classroom at school.

■ 2. Design a wall hanging for a small child's room. Use Roman minuscules, and decorate the hanging appropriately.

■ 3. Write and illustrate a book for primary children. Print the text in the Roman alphabet.

Name _____

Roman with Serif

One writing surface used by the ancient Greeks and Romans was stone. Painstakingly, they chipped and chiseled names, dates, and messages into the hard, smooth face of granite or marble. Letters with no ornamentation and few curved lines were easier to cut into stone, and so many of the early alphabets consisted of letters that were simple and straight. Today, type styles are identified as being **Roman**, meaning straight, or *Italic*, meaning slanted.

According to some authorities, the Romans wanted their carved letters to cast shadows. For this reason, they added **serifs**, or short, light lines that projected at an angle from the upper and lower ends of their letter strokes. Today, type is still described as having serifs or as being **sans serif**, which means "without serifs." Sans serif type is also called **Gothic**.

To be formed correctly, the calligraphic serif must be made in three strokes. For very small letters or in an informal writing style, the serif may be made with one cross-stroke.

Regardless of the method used, the serif must have a straight edge. The serifs on Roman minuscules go only one way. Be sure to learn the correct serif for each letter

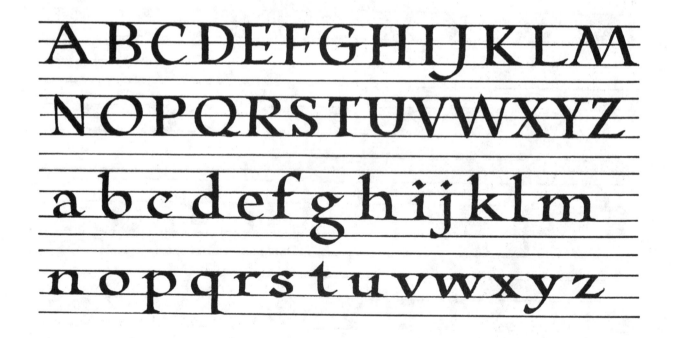

Activities

● 1. The word **minuscule** is in common use in English today but not to indicate a lowercase letter. Look up this word. What is its other meaning?

■ 2. Collect examples of Roman letters in handwritten or typeset material or from photographs of statues or monuments. Classify these examples as serif or sans serif.

▲ 3. Obtain some moist clay, form it into a block, and allow this block to dry. With a sharp tool, chisel a proverb or saying into the clay block.

★ 4. Make a chart showing the separate strokes needed to create each of the Roman majuscules and minuscules pictured above. Number these strokes to indicate their order.

Name _____

Roman Letters

Derived from the Greek alphabet, Roman majuscules are the basis for all capital letters. They were first painted on stone by Roman scribes who used a brush and a sweeping movement much like that used by sign painters today. Ancient writers used mallets and chisels to inscribe letters of this type on the aqueducts and the theater and forum built during the reign of the emperor, Trajan (A.D. 53-117). The Romans also used these letters on their bridges, coins, tokens, and stone distance markers.

When Roman scribes became aware of papyrus and parchment, they fashioned pens from the hollow reeds that grew along the banks of the Tiber River. Writing with a pen on paper was not nearly so difficult as chiseling in stone had been, and this change in writing surfaces made it possible for the scribes to be more flexible in their writing style. They began to vary their alphabet and even to add minuscules.

Activities

1. The Roman emperor Trajan was widely recognized for his abilities as a military organizer and a civic administrator. He is remembered largely because of his immense efforts to build and restore Rome. Read about this ancient ruler. Then write a one-act play based on a single episode in his life or on a series of his accomplishments.

2. Draw a map showing some of the areas in which the Romans might have placed their alphabetical inscriptions.

3. Design a name marker for your school using Roman majuscules.

4. Using a sharp knife, cut off the end of a tongue depressor or Popsicle stick. Write the Roman alphabet first with the uncut, rounded end and then with the flat end. Compare these two writing instruments. Describe the differences and difficulties you encounter in writing with each one.

Free Roman

Free Roman is a very informal style of writing both the Roman majuscule and the Roman minuscule. In this writing style, the letters are more rounded, and they sit on the line at a variety of angles. To create these whimsical letters, first draw their outlines and then shade or fill in the wider parts.

Free Roman Majuscules

ABCDEFGH
IJKLMNOPQ
RSTUVWXYZ

Free Roman Minuscules

abcdefghijklm
nopqrstuvwxyz

Activities

■ 1. Make a list of the ways in which you could use this informal writing style.
▲ 2. Use Free Roman letters on a poster.
▲ 3. Create a newspaper or magazine ad in which you use Free Roman letters.
■ 4. Compare the Roman and Free Roman styles of writing. Create a chart on which you briefly describe and illustrate the ways in which they are alike or different and on which you list some appropriate uses for each style.

Name _____

Chancery Cursive

Because Roman letters had to be formed individually, with straight lines and great care, writing in this style took a long time and was impractical for both record keeping and manuscript copying. As an alternative, a scribe named Ludovico degli Arrighi developed a more connected and flowing script and, in 1522, advocated its use in *La Operina,* the first handwriting manual for popular use. Because the style was developed in Italy, it was called **Italic**. Because Ludovico was a Vatican chancery scribe, it was also called **Chancery Cursive**. This script became one of the most popular writing styles during the Italian Renaissance.

Chancery Cursive letters are very different from Roman ones. You will remember that Roman letters are straight, almost square, and are well spaced. They are formed by holding the pen at a 30- to 35-degree angle. Roman majuscules are nine pen widths high, and Roman minuscules are five pen widths high. Chancery letters, on the other hand, are slightly slanted, narrow, and so close together that they appear, at times, to be connected. They are formed by holding the pen at a 45-degree angle, which yields a line that is very thick in some places and very thin in others.

To write in Chancery Cursive, hold your pen at a 45-degree angle and keep the entire edge of your pen nib in contact with the paper.

Chancery Cursive capital letters are only seven pen widths high. Ascenders and descenders on lowercase letters extend five full pen widths above or below the middle writing space.

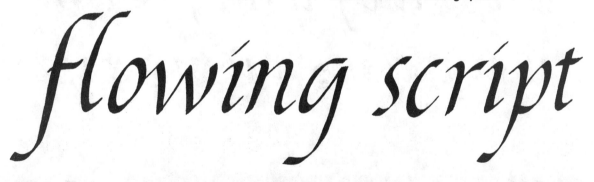

Activities

▲ 1. Using your T-square, make a ruled guide sheet to use under plain white paper with each of your pen nibs. Label each sheet with the appropriate pen name, letter, and number so that you will know when to use it.

▬ 2. Locate a paragraph containing at least seventy-five words. The first or second paragraph on this page will work fine. Ask a friend to time you while you copy the paragraph you have chosen *neatly* on a separate sheet of paper using the manuscript alphabet (see page 87). Record your time. Then ask a friend to time you while you recopy this same paragraph *neatly* using the cursive alphabet (see page 87). Again record your time. Compare the two times. Which alphabet do you prefer to use? Why?

Name _____

Chancery Cursive
(continued)

Chancery Cursive lowercase letters are written in the middle space. As was true of Roman minuscules, Chancery Cursive lowercase letters are five pen widths high. The parts of letters like *b*, *d*, *f*, *h*, *l*, and *t* that extend *above* the middle writing space are called **ascenders**. The parts of letters like *f*, *j*, *p*, *q*, and *y* that extend *below* this middle space are called **descenders**. Chancery Cursive ascenders and descenders extend a full five pen widths above or below the middle writing space. Properly formed Chancery Cursive capital letters are only seven pen widths high, two pen widths shorter than Roman majuscules.

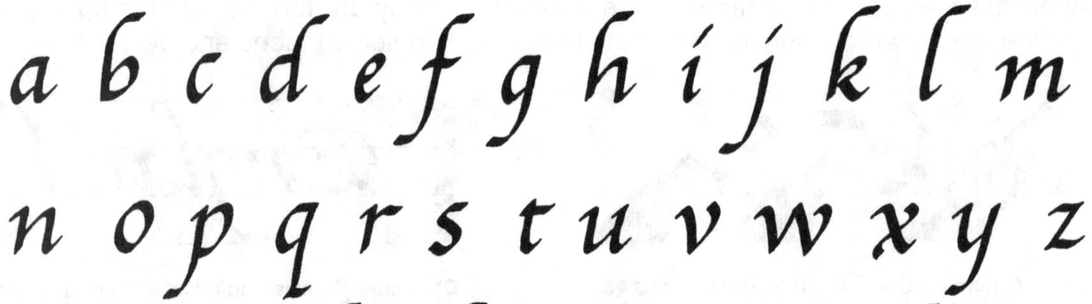

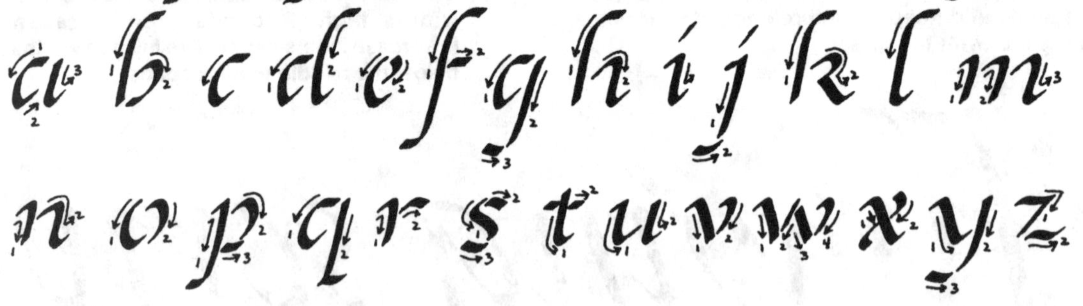

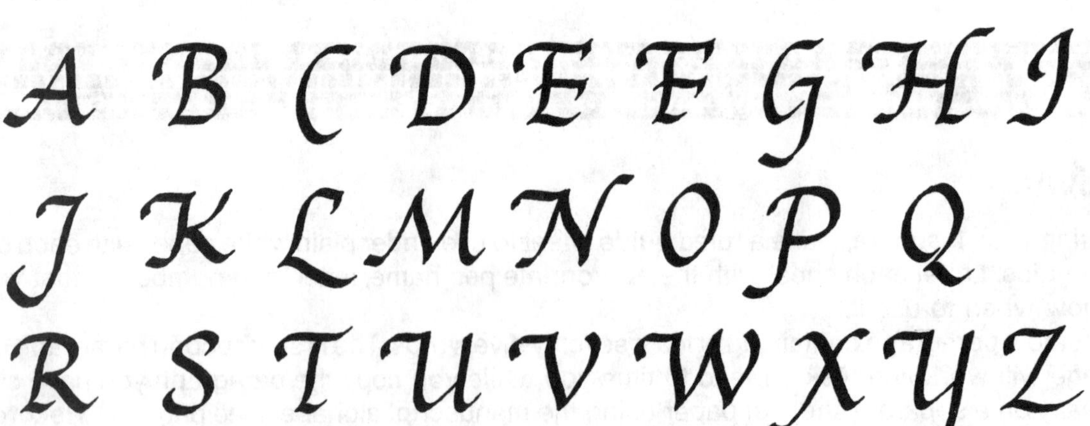

a b c d e f g h i j k l m
n o p q r s t u v w x y z

a b c d e f g h i j k l m
n o p q r s t u v w x y z

A B C D E F G H I
J K L M N O P Q
R S T U V W X Y Z

Name _____

Chancery Cursive Lowercase Letters

As you practice the following exercises, hold your pen at a 45-degree angle, keep the entire edge of your pen nib in contact with the paper, and space the letters and lines evenly.

ı ı ı ı ı ı u u u u u ı ı ı ı ı ı n n n n

ı ı ı ı ı u u u u n n n ı ı u u n n

i j l u n i j l i j l u n m h n m h n

r r y y ı ı o o ı ı o o e e ı ı e e moon

m m m m u u u u a a a l l l l l

Name _____

Chancery Cursive Lowercase Letters
(continued)

Continue practicing these lowercase italic letters until you have mastered them. If you need more practice after you finish this page, use additional sheets of paper.

a o v o e a a c d d g g g quit

_____
_____
_____

b b h h k k ff t t back flat

_____
_____
_____

r r p p s s v v w w x x y z z

_____
_____
_____

After you have mastered these individual lowercase italic letters, try putting some of them together in words.

❖❖❖❖❖❖❖❖❖❖❖❖❖❖❖❖❖❖❖❖❖❖❖❖❖❖❖❖❖❖❖❖❖❖❖❖❖❖

Activities

● 1. Practice these strokes, letters, and words on another sheet of paper.

★ 2. Analyze your calligraphy. Why are the letters very thick in some places and very thin in others?

Name _____

Chancery Cursive Capital Letters

When you feel that you have mastered individual lowercase letters and can combine them to write words, practice the capital letters and numbers.

A B C D E F G H I

J K L M N O P Q

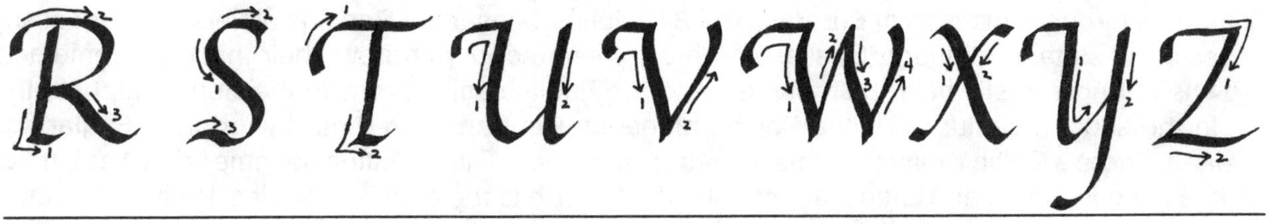

R S T U V W X Y Z

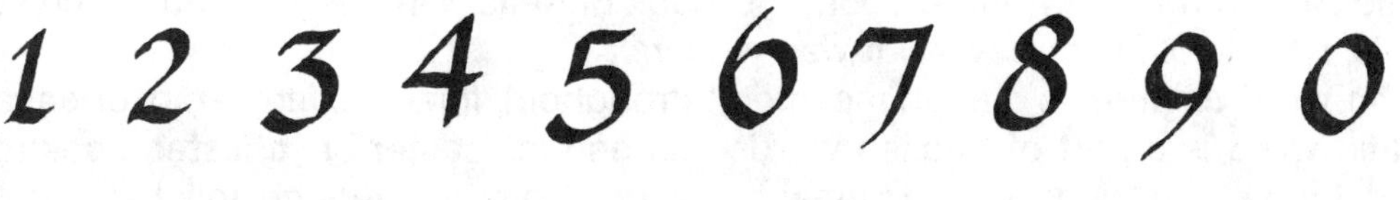

1 2 3 4 5 6 7 8 9 0

Activities

■ 1. Collect samples of old-fashioned and modern italic letters in handwritten or typeset material.
■ 2. Compose a poem. Then copy it in italic letters.
■ 3. Design a party invitation. Write the text in italic script.

Name _____

Uncial

In the more than one thousand years between the development of the Roman alphabet and the appearance of Chancery Cursive, many writing styles flourished. Among these styles was **Uncial**.

Uncial is an alphabet of somewhat rounded Roman majuscules, called **uncials**. These letters have few ascenders and descenders, and they do not extend far above or below the middle writing space. When these letters are written properly, a lot of space is left between one line and the next.

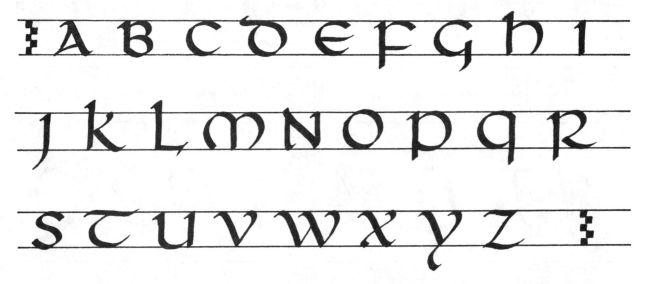

The origin of the name uncial is uncertain, but **uncia** is a Latin word meaning "twelfth part or one-twelfth of a pound" and is closely related to our word **ounce**. It was also the name of a bronze coin of the ancient Roman republic.

During the first century B.C. and the first and second centuries A.D., the Romans extended their influence throughout much of Europe. In 54 B.C., Julius Caesar led Roman soldiers in a successful invasion of Britain. Although Caesar and his soldiers soon withdrew, their influence remained. Towns in England still bear Latin names, and the English still write with the Roman alphabet.

In the second century A.D., the Roman alphabet was transported northward from England to Ireland. There a Celtic variation of this alphabet developed. This variation became known as Uncial. It was used in Greek and Latin manuscripts of the fourth to the eighth centuries. Perhaps the most famous manuscript written in Celtic uncials is the Book of Kells.

Activities

● 1. Find out about the Celts. Who were they? Where did they live? When were they there?

■ 2. Do some research to learn more about the Book of Kells. Write a report in which you explain what it is, who wrote it, and when it was written.

▆ 3. The Latin word **castrum** is a noun meaning "stronghold, fort, fortified camp, or encampment." This Latin word is a part of English words that end in **-caster** or **-chester**. Look at a map of England. Find some towns whose names show this Roman influence. In what part of England are most of the ones that end in **-caster** located? In what part of England are most of the ones that end in **-chester** located? Why?

▲ 4. Find out more about the Roman Empire. On a map of Europe, trace its growth. When did it exist? How long did it last? How far did its influence spread? Who were some of its important political and military leaders?

Name _____

Scribes and Books

The Egyptians, Greeks, and Romans all employed **scribes** to write their important documents and copy their books; and this practice continued through the Middle Ages and early Renaissance. These scribes would sit at desks in small rooms, called **scriptoriums**, and laboriously copy manuscripts by hand.

One of the most beautiful books ever written in this manner is the Book of Kells. This book was found in an ancient monastery near Kells, a small town in Meath County, Ireland, that lies northwest of Dublin near Navan. Copied in Irish majuscule script (a kind of Uncial), this book is a beautifully illuminated manuscript of the Latin Gospels, with notes on local history, and is believed to have been written in the eighth century.

Activities

● 1. Set up a **scriptorium** in your classroom for students to use as a place to practice calligraphy.

■ 2. The Book of Kells was found at an ancient monastery near Kells, Ireland. What is a **monastery**? Find out about and report on monasteries and the role monks played as scribes.

▲ 3. Copy a nursery rhyme or other poem in Uncial, and decorate the page.

Name _____

Humanist Bookhand

   A beautiful writing style was developed in France during the reign of Charlemagne (A.D. 768-814); but for some unknown reason, it was soon forgotten. During the fourteenth century, scribes looking over old manuscripts rediscovered this style. Mistakenly assuming that it was the same alphabet used by the ancient Romans, they paired it with Roman majuscules, made some subtle changes, and used it to copy books. Because these scribes were called Humanists, the alphabet they used became known as **Humanist Bookhand**.

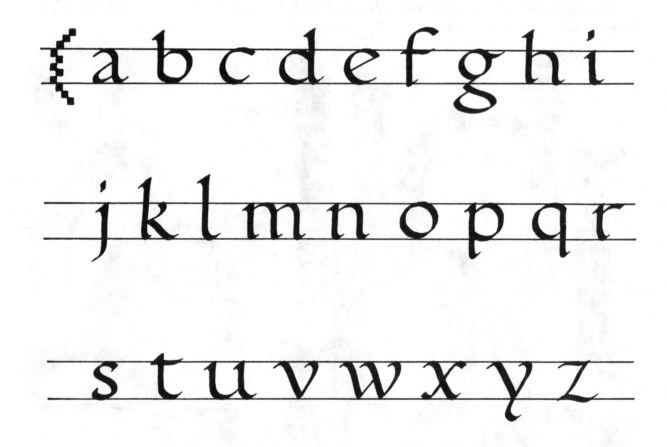

Activities

■ 1. Do some research to learn more about the Humanists. With what period of history are they associated? Why were they given this name? On what did they focus their artistic and scholarly attention? What period of history did they revere? Summarize your findings in a brief report or moderate a panel discussion in which several students, acting as Humanists, explain and discuss their interests and beliefs.

▲2. Pretend that you are a scribe. Copy one paragraph from a book in Humanist Bookhand.

■ 3. Compare the alphabet pictured here with the manuscript alphabet on page 87. Which letters are alike? Which letters are different? In what ways are they different?

■ 4. Compare the alphabet pictured here with the Roman alphabet on page 90. Do you see why scribes might mistake one for the other? Make a chart on which you show some of the basic similarities and differences between these two writing styles. Look carefully. Don't be fooled like the Humanist scribes were!

Name _____

Carolingian

During the eighth and ninth centuries, the Carolingians ruled France. This dynasty began with the reign of Charlemagne in 768 and ended one hundred and twenty years later with Louis V, who was king of France from 986 to 987. An alphabet developed in France during this time was named for this ruling family and is called **Carolingian**.

a b c d e f g h i j k l m n

o p q r s t u v w x y z

A B C D E F G H I

J K L M N O P Q R

S T U V W X Y Z

Activities

1. Find out more about the Carolingians. What rulers did this group include? How did this family come to power? What event or series of events caused them to lose power? What family succeeded them as rulers of France? Write a report about the Carolingians. Include a Carolingian family tree as one of your illustrations.

2. Find out about life in France during the reign of the Carolingians. Write a series of paragraphs or draw and label a series of pictures to explain the clothing people wore, the houses they lived in, the work they did, and the amusements they enjoyed.

Name _____

Lombardic

The Lombards were an ancient Germanic tribe that invaded northern Italy in A.D. 568 and established a kingdom there. This kingdom flourished during the seventh and eighth centuries, until the Lombards were defeated by Charlemagne in A.D. 774. Despite this defeat, the region of Italy that extends from the Swiss border to the Po River and from the Ticino River to the Mincio River is known as Lombardy. It was in this region that the alphabet known as **Lombardic** developed during the twelfth century and was widely used for two hundred years. These decorative letters are created by drawing their outlines and then shading or filling in the wider parts.

Activities

▲ 1. The English word **gonfalon**, meaning "a flag or banner that hangs from a crosspiece or frame," comes from the Italian word **gonfalone**, meaning "the ensign of one of the medieval republics of Italy." During the Middle Ages, Italy was not one nation, but many nations, or states, each governed by a noble and his army. Each one of these nobles had his own **gonfalone,** which he hung in his palace and which his soldiers carried to identify them when they rode in battle or parade. Use Lombardic letters to create a gonfalon—an identifying banner—for your family or school.

■ 2. Find out more about Lombardy. What was life in this region like during the twelfth century? Write
◉ a report in which you compare life in this region during the twelfth century with life in this region today. In what ways are they alike? In what ways are they different? Which way of life do you prefer? Why?

Name _____

Black Letter

The Gothic, Old English, or **Black Letter** (as most modern books call it) alphabet is characterized by heavy black vertical lines, from which it gets its name. This alphabet is both dignified and decorative. For this reason, it was widely used in both churches and courts throughout Europe during the twelfth through the fifteenth centuries. In fact, when Johann Gutenberg printed the Bible in about 1437, he used this letter style.

Activities

1. Johann Gutenberg (*ca.* 1400-1468) is credited with being the first European to print with movable type. Find out more about Gutenberg. Where did he live? With whom did he go into partnership? How did this business venture work out? How did Gutenberg's printing process work? What organization finally recognized and rewarded Gutenberg financially for his printing achievements? Why?

2. In 1884, Ottmar Mergenthaler patented the first Linotype typesetting machine. Do some research to learn about Mergenthaler and his invention. In a report, explain how it changed the typesetting process. How had type been set before Mergenthaler's invention? How is most type set today?

3. From a substance that can be easily cut (for example, linoleum), carve some letters. Glue these to individual wooden blocks of uniform size. Print by pressing these blocks, letter side down, on an inked stamp pad and then on paper. Compare your printing process with that used by Gutenberg and that made possible by the Linotype machine and by the rotary and web presses.

4. There are different types of printing presses. Among them are the rotary and web presses. Find out about these two types of presses. Then make a table or chart on which you compare the process invented by Gutenberg with these two more modern printing processes.

5. Copying by hand and printing from plates are two methods of producing books. On a chart, list the advantages and disadvantages of each method. Consider such factors as accuracy, beauty, cost, readability, the time required, and the uniformity of product. Then explain which method *you* think is best and tell why you think so.

Name _____

Black Letter Minuscules

Black Letter minuscules look difficult, but they are really quite easy because all of them are made with only three basic types of pen strokes.

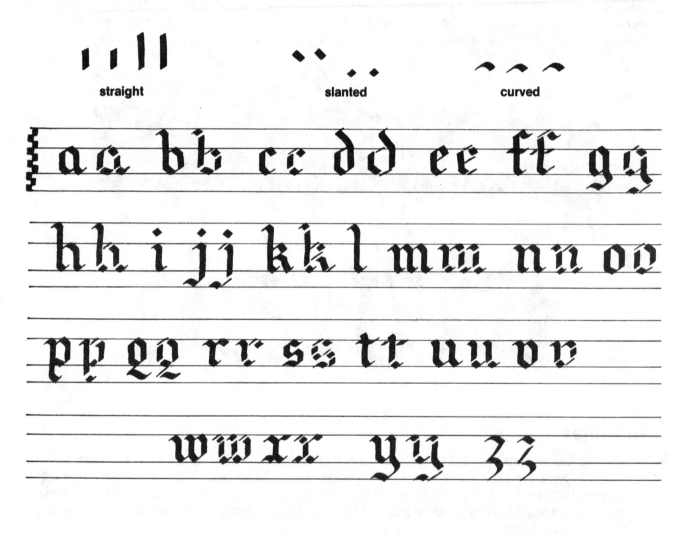

straight   **slanted**   **curved**

Activities

▲ 1. With your T-square and the pen tip you plan to use for Black Letter, make a ruled guide sheet to use when you write this alphabet.

● 2. Practice making the three basic types of pen strokes that are used to make Black Letter minuscules.

● 3. Use your guide sheet to practice writing the letters of this alphabet. Practice the letters one at a time. Write a complete line of one letter before you go on to the next letter.

■ 4. This alphabet is often used today on awards and certificates. If possible, obtain several of these documents and compare them. Decide which features you like best. Then design an award incorporating these features.

▲ 5. Plan a party. Use the Black Letter alphabet to write invitations and name tags or place cards for the party.

Name _____

Black Letter Majuscules

Elaborate Black Letter majuscules add elegance to any manuscript. They are made with the same pen strokes that you used for Black Letter minuscules.

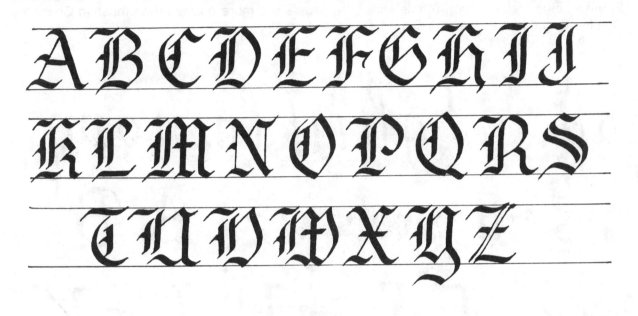

Black Letter is written so that letters within a single word are close together, but there is as much as a full letter width of space between separate words. Here is an example of words written in this alphabet.

> Kingdoms are but cares,
> State devoid of stay;
> Riches are ready snares
> And hasten to decay.
>
> HENRY VI
> 1421-1471

Activities

1. Many modern typefaces have been created to imitate old-fashioned handwriting styles. Collect and display similar examples of modern type created in imitation of older calligraphic styles. If possible, label each item in your display with the name of the modern typeface and the name of the old-fashioned style on which it is based.

2. Select one example in the collection you put together for activity 1. Compare each letter in that example with the same letter shown on a related calligraphic chart in this book or elsewhere. In what ways are they alike? In what ways are they different?

Name _____

Batarde

Over the years, several italic writing styles evolved. One of these is **Batarde**, a script developed during the seventeenth century by the French. Batarde is called a **round hand**, which means that most of the lines used to write it are curved rather than straight or angular. In the modern English commercial version of this script, the letters are more pointed than those in Chancery Cursive, and the lines are somewhat less slanted.

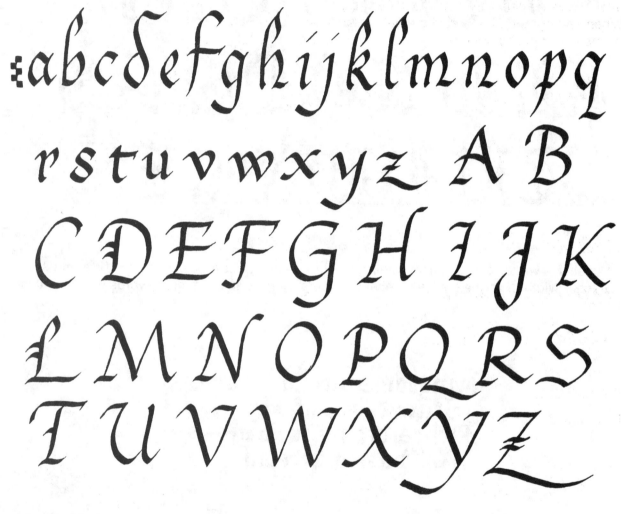

Activities

▲ 1. On a sheet of parchment or other fine paper, copy several epigrams, homilies, or other memorable quotations using Chancery Cursive or Batarde.

▲ 2. For Mother's Day or some other similar special occasion, make a greeting card, scroll, or plaque. Copy an appropriate sentiment on a sheet of parchment or other fine quality paper using Chancery Cursive or Batarde. Add decorative designs and small illustrations. Fold or roll your creation to make a card or scroll. Frame it to make a plaque.

■ 3. Design a wall hanging for a kitchen. Include a message written in Chancery Cursive or Batarde. Follow your design to create a hanging printed on parchment or other relatively stiff paper, or embroidered on linen or other fine fabric.

Name _____

English Roundhand

English Roundhand, or Copperplate, is a script long used by engravers for formal announcements. It is characterized by round letters and lines of sharply contrasting thickness. This effect is achieved by using a pen with a very fine point and varying the pressure on it. Pressure is applied heavily during the downstroke to thicken these lines.

The pen most frequently used for Roundhand is called an **elbow pen,** because the tip holder is attached to the pen staff at an elbow-like angle. When writing, the pen is held so that the staff points over the shoulder of the writing arm.

A special pen called an elbow pen is used to write Roundhand.

English Roundhand, or Copperplate, is a script long used by en-gravers for formal announce-ments and for delicate and tasteful invitations.

Activities

● 1. Practice these pen strokes and Roundhand letters.

llllllll eeeeeee uuuuu ffffffff
ooooooo aaaaaaaaaa mmmm
hhhhh ttttt ccccc bbbbbbb

■ 2. This style is also called **Copperplate** because it was based on writing engraved in copper with a burin. Find out about the engraving process. Of what steps does it consist? What tools does an engraver use? Summarize what you learn on an illustrated chart.

★ 3. Explain why the engraving process might yield lines of sharply contrasting thickness.

Name _____

English Roundhand
(continued)

Of all the alphabets you have learned about thus far, English Roundhand is most like the cursive alphabet you use in school. The greatest single difference is that the lines used to form cursive letters are all of the same thickness while the lines used to form Roundhand letters are of differing thicknesses.

Aa Bb Cc Dd Ee Ff
Gg Hh Ii Jj Kk Ll
Mm Nn Oo Pp Qq
Rr Ss Tt Uu Vv Ww
Xx Yy Zz

Activities

● 1. One at a time, practice making the letters of this alphabet. Write a complete line of one letter before you go on to the next letter. Start with the minuscules. Once you have mastered them, go on to the majuscules. Then, put letters together to form words.

■ 2. Because Roundhand is so much like cursive, it can easily be used for writing letters and for making final copies of handwritten school assignments. Use Roundhand in one of these ways.

★ 3. Compare the cursive and Roundhand alphabets. Point out the similarities and differences between these two writing styles in an illustrated paper or on a chart. Be specific, and use actual letter examples.

Name _____

Illumination

Illumination is decoration of manuscripts by hand. During the Middle Ages, monks and scribes decorated their manuscripts with fancy initials, delightful borders, and miniature pictures painted in brilliant colors. Strictly speaking, to be classed as illumination and not merely decoration, these designs had to include gold, which was painstakingly applied and then burnished until it glowed.

Often, as part of illumination, the first letter on a page or of a special word was enlarged, written in a different color, or decorated with a design or drawing. Sometimes, these letters were merely enlarged calligraphic letters that had been made more ornate. Other times, these letters were decorated with actual pictures that might include flowers or foliage. Illuminated initials were overlapped to form monograms. They were also created from human or animal forms.

Illumination should not be gaudy. It should be closely related to both the subject and the feeling of the text and should help to make its meaning more clear. Even decorative borders should reflect the message being imparted or the story being told by the text.

Activities

▲ 1. Write a paragraph in which you use at least one illuminated letter.

▲ 2. Use calligraphy to rewrite a fairy tale or other familiar story. When you write, leave plenty of room around the edges. After the ink dries, add a border that illustrates the story.

■ 3. Design your own monogram.

■ 4. Use black ink to create a monogram and a border that reflects some of your special interests on a piece of high-quality white paper. Turn this design into personalized stationery by having it photocopied on the paper of your choice at a local print shop. If you wish, use colored inks to fill in some of the open areas in the photocopied design.

★ 5. Go to the library. Ask the research librarian to help you find an illuminated book. Study it carefully and notice the letter and drawing styles and the colors that have been used. Evaluate the illumination against the criteria outlined above. Explain why you think that it is or is not suited to the text.

Name _____

Posttest

Indicate which alphabet you would use for each of the listed items by writing a letter on each line.

_____ 1. wedding announcement   A.   Black Letter

_____ 2. award or certificate   B.   Chancery Cursive

_____ 3. invitation to a tea party   C.   English Roundhand

_____ 4. book for primary students   D.   Roman

Write **T** in front of each statement that is true. Write **F** in front of each statement that is false.

_____ 5. Posture is very important to the calligrapher.

_____ 6. Felt-tipped pens write as well as pens with metal tips.

_____ 7. Johann Gutenberg changed the lives of scribes.

_____ 8. The cursive hand we use in school today is similar to an older handwriting style called English Roundhand.

_____ 9. Free Roman would be a good alphabet to use on a wedding announcement.

_____ 10. The original plain Roman alphabet is no longer in use.

Write the correct answer on each line.

11. Each movement of a pen is called a _____ .

12. For a handwritten message to be readable, uniform _____ must be left between words.

13. When you write in calligraphy, the paper you are writing on should be _____ , and you should hold your pen at a _____ angle.

14. To make filling a reservoir pen easy, you should buy your ink in a bottle with a _____ .

15. Hand decoration of an individual letter or of a manuscript page is called _____ .

Answer Key

Page 80, Pretest

1.	F	11.	H
2.	E	12.	I
3.	B	13.	M
4.	C	14.	K
5.	A	15.	L
6.	D	16.	R
7.	G	17.	P
8.	O	18.	N
9.	Q	19.	J
10.	T	20.	S

Page 110, Posttest

1. C
2. A
3. B
4. D
5. T
6. F
7. T
8. T
9. F
10. F
11. stroke
12. space
13. straight; high
14. dropper
15. illumination

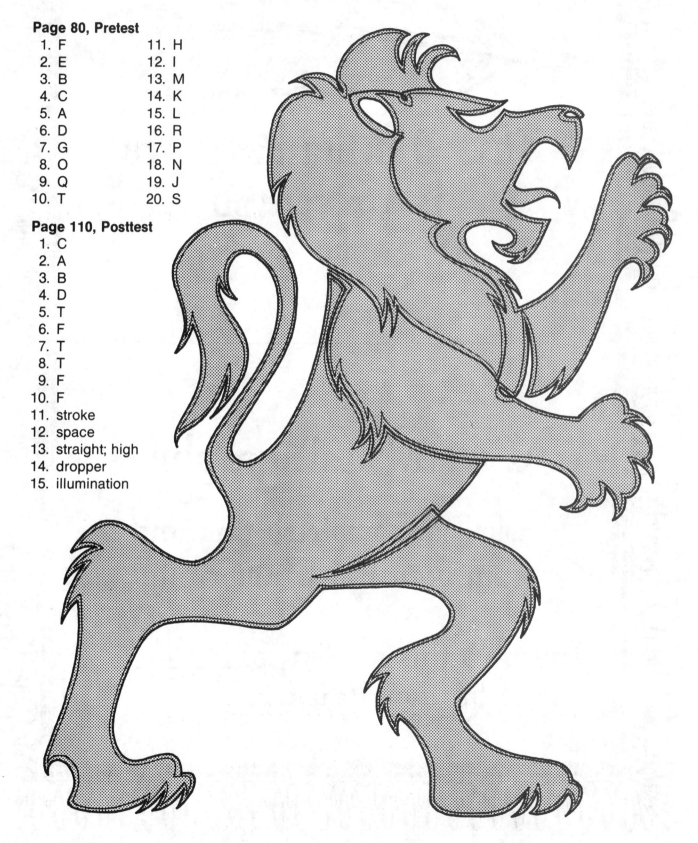

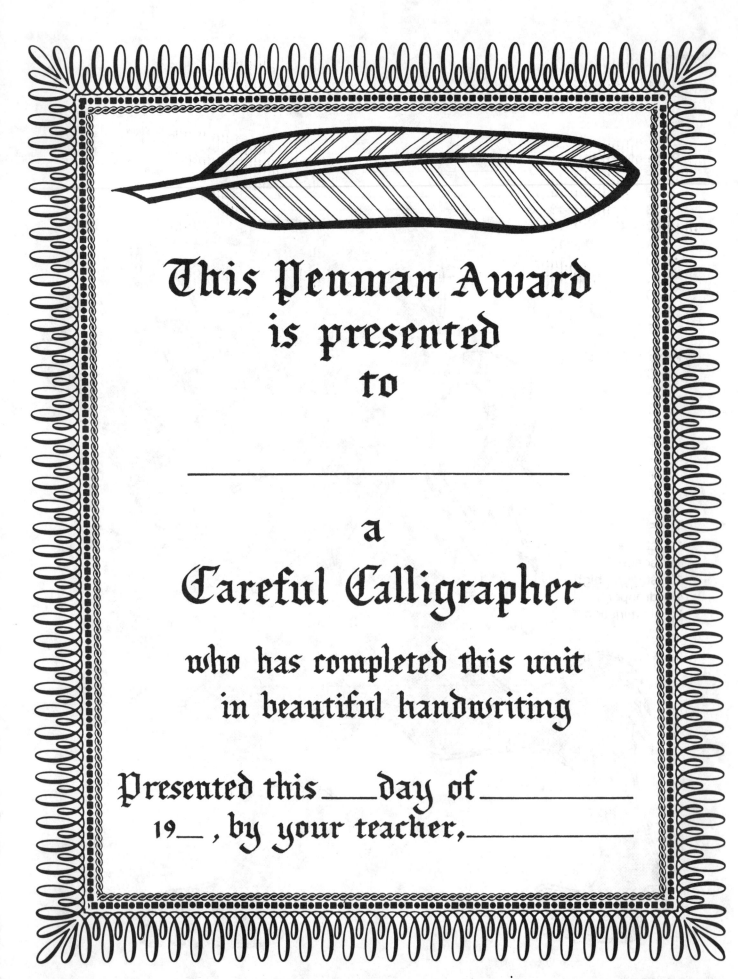

This Penman Award
is presented
to

_____

a
Careful Calligrapher

who has completed this unit
in beautiful handwriting

Presented this ____ day of _____
19___ , by your teacher, _____